THE JOY OF

ENCOURAGEMENT

Unlock *the* Power *of* Building Others Up

Dr. David Jeremiah

with Dr. David Jeremiah

CONTENTS

ABOUT
DR. DAVID JEREMIAH
AND TURNING POINT

D r. David Jeremiah is the founder of Turning Point, a ministry committed to providing Christians with sound Bible teaching relevant to today's changing times through radio and television broadcasts, audio series, books, and rallies. Dr. Jeremiah's common-sense teaching on topics such as family, prayer, worship, angels, and biblical prophecy forms the foundation of Turning Point.

David and his wife, Donna, reside in El Cajon, California, where he serves as the senior pastor of Shadow Mountain Community Church. David and Donna have four children and ten grandchildren.

In 1982, Dr. Jeremiah brought the same solid teaching to San Diego television that he shares weekly with his congregation. Shortly thereafter, Turning Point expanded its ministry to radio. Dr. Jeremiah's inspiring messages can now be heard worldwide on radio, television, and the Internet.

Because Dr. Jeremiah desires to know his listening audience, he travels nationwide holding ministry rallies and spiritual enrichment conferences that touch the hearts and lives of many people. According to Dr. Jeremiah, "At some point in time, everyone reaches a turning point; and for every person, that moment is unique, an experience to hold onto forever. There's so much changing in today's world that sometimes it's difficult to choose the right path. Turning Point offers people an understanding of God's Word as well as the opportunity to make a difference in their lives."

Dr. Jeremiah has authored numerous books, including *Escape the Coming Night* (Revelation), *The Handwriting on the Wall* (Daniel), *Overcoming Loneliness, Grand Parenting, The Joy of Encouragement, Prayer—The Great Adventure, God in You* (Holy Spirit), *Gifts from God* (Parenting), *Jesus' Final Warning, When Your World Falls Apart, Slaying the Giants in Your Life, My Heart's Desire, Sanctuary, Life Wide Open, Searching for Heaven on Earth, The Secret of the Light, Captured by Grace, Discover Paradise, Grace Givers, Why the Nativity?, Signs of Life, The 12 Ways of Christmas, 1 Minute a Day, What in the World Is Going On?,* and *The Coming Economic Armageddon.*

ABOUT THIS
STUDY GUIDE

The purpose of this Turning Point study guide is to reinforce Dr. David Jeremiah's dynamic, in-depth teaching and to aid the reader in applying biblical truth to his or her daily life. This study guide is designed to be used in conjunction with Dr. Jeremiah's *The Joy of Encouragement* audio series, but it may also be used by itself for personal or group study.

STRUCTURE OF THE LESSONS

Each lesson is based on one of the messages in the *The Joy of Encouragement* compact disc series and focuses on specific passages in the Bible. Each lesson is composed of the following elements:

- *Outline*

The outline at the beginning of the lesson gives a clear, concise picture of the topic being studied and provides a helpful framework for readers as they listen to Dr. Jeremiah's teaching.

- *Overview*

The overview summarizes Dr. Jeremiah's teaching on the passage being studied in the lesson. Readers should refer to the Scripture passages in their own Bibles as they study the overview. Unless otherwise indicated, Scripture verses quoted are taken from the New King James Version.

- *Application*

This section contains a variety of questions designed to help readers dig deeper into the lesson and the Scriptures, and to apply the lesson to their daily lives. For Bible study groups or Sunday school classes, these questions will provide a springboard for group discussion and interaction.

- *Did You Know?*

This section presents a fascinating fact, historical note, or insight that adds a point of interest to the preceding lesson.

Using This Guide for Group Study

The lessons in this study guide are suitable for Sunday school classes, small-group studies, elective Bible studies, or home Bible study groups. Each person in the group should have his or her own study guide.

When possible, the study guide should be used with the corresponding compact disc series. You may wish to assign the study guide lesson as homework prior to the meeting of the group and then use the meeting time to listen to the CD and discuss the lesson.

For Continuing Study

For a complete listing of Dr. Jeremiah's materials for personal and group study call 1-800-947-1993, go online to www.DavidJeremiah.org, or write to: Turning Point, P.O. Box 3838, San Diego, CA 92163.

Dr. Jeremiah's *Turning Point* program is currently heard or viewed around the world on radio, television, and the Internet in English. *Momento Decisivo*, the Spanish translation of Dr. Jeremiah's messages, can be heard on radio in every Spanish speaking country in the world. The television broadcast is also broadcast by satellite throughout the Middle East with Arabic subtitles.

Contact Turning Point for radio and television program times and stations in your area. Or visit our website at www.DavidJeremiah.org.

THE
JOY OF
ENCOURAGEMENT

INTRODUCTION

If you follow sports at all, you know that regardless of the game, home-field advantage is a legitimate factor in determining the outcome of contests. Whether it's a college basketball game in an arena, a football game played in the chilly outdoors, or a baseball game played in the warmth of spring sunshine, the home team has an advantage that is statistically significant.

So what is it about playing at home that can spur teams with less talent to outplay their visiting foes? Is it intimate knowledge of the playing surface? Maybe. Is it the comfort of not having to travel and of sleeping in one's own bed? That could be a factor too.

But the real answer to why home-field advantage is what it is really has nothing to do with the teams—it has to do with the spectators.

A hometown crowd has the power to mentally make or break athletes. A succession of boos can discourage an opposing player to a slump. And conversely, the cheers and chants and encouragement of a hometown crowd to one of its beloved players or teams can (and does) push them to victory more times than not.

If the magnified cheers of strangers can push a professional athlete beyond their limits to victory, think about the impact that positive, focused encouragement by close friends and family could have on someone. It would give them more than victory in a ball game—it would give them victory in life.

Then why are we so hesitant to offer an encouraging word to one another? Maybe because we are so discouraged ourselves! But thankfully we don't have to turn to modern psychiatry or self-help books to put us in a positive direction. God is the author of encouragement and His Word is full of examples and insights to help us turn our lives around.

In *The Joy of Encouragement,* we are going to delve into Scripture so that we can build this critical attribute into our arsenal. The Bible shows us that encouragement is available in so many different places.

We can find it in solitude and in songs. We can find it in our marriages. We can find it in the church. And most of all, we can find it in the Gospel! After all, there is no more encouraging news than the knowledge that we have been reconciled to God by the work of Jesus Christ on the cross.

And there is no shortage of places where we need to be vigilant encouragers. We should be the most outspoken cheerleaders for our spouses and children. We should edify the church that Christ has died for at all times. We should try to lift our friends up when they are down. These are all roles that are commanded of us in God's Word if we are to be faithful followers of Christ.

And there is not a set way to be a light to someone in their darkness. Sometimes all it takes is a few words. Sometimes all it takes is a hug. Sometimes it takes the effort to sit down and write someone a letter about how much they mean to you. The point is that it isn't complex; simple actions and words can mean a world of difference to people. We just need to be willing to be there.

So what are we waiting for? Let's go to God's Word with open minds and hearts so that we can not only be encouraged in our own lives and faith but also so that we can share that joy with those around us.

EVERYBODY IS A SOMEBODY

Selected Scriptures

In this lesson we learn why encouragement is an indispensable ingredient in every human life.

OUTLINE

God's creation is complementary: Humans need oxygen and plants produce it; plants need carbon dioxide and humans exhale it. Likewise, because every person is important and needs encouragement, God has given every person the ability to be an encourager.

   I.   **Encouragement Is the Urgent Need of Our Day**

  II.   **Encouragement Is the Unique Priority of God**

 III.   **Encouragement Is the Underlying Purpose of Our Bible**

 IV.   **Encouragement Is the Uncommon Opportunity to Begin a Never-Ending Process**

An airline pilot received a diagnosis of brain cancer with a 50 percent chance of surviving more than five years. He wrote a letter to a newspaper columnist describing how his "family" of fellow pilots rallied around him and began to encourage him. He received stacks of cards and letters in the mail, and he and his family were sent on a beautiful vacation trip—all expenses paid. He said that the "friend therapy" he received was a major factor in his surviving cancer.

I don't know that I had ever heard that phrase before—"friend therapy"—but the more I thought about it, the better it seemed to be a perfect way to describe encouragement. Friend therapy is when people come alongside to encourage us when we are going through difficult times. In the New Testament, the word "to encourage" is a combination of the Greek word *para*, which means "alongside of," and *kaleo*, which means "to call"—*parakaleo* (the noun "encouragement" is *paraklesis*).

So to encourage is to be called alongside someone. I think of one person coming along and putting his arm around another's shoulder—partly for support, partly just to impart a human touch, but always to strengthen and build up. I believe there are four reasons God wants us to make encouragement a high priority in the body of Christ.

ENCOURAGEMENT IS THE URGENT NEED OF OUR DAY

I used to believe the philosophy that one generation's problems were no different than another's—that life's problems just repeat themselves from one generation to another. But I don't believe that anymore. The kinds of problems the present generation faces are unique—no previous generation has ever faced them before. Things that were only imagined in past generations have now become realities for us. We have crises in our generation of almost every conceivable kind: crime and prison crises, drug abuse crises, national debt crises, health care systems/Medicare crises, sexually transmitted disease crises (including AIDS), adolescent suicide crises, liability and litigation crises, ethics crises at every level both personal and public—and on and on. While some of these problems have existed in the past, the scary thing is how in our generation they are all present and are increasing at an alarming rate.

Not only do we have all of these problems, we have one problem that is even larger: No one seems to know what to do about all the problems we have! Regardless of what we hear coming from Washington DC, the problems our society faces are not getting fixed. And often when a solution is tried, it creates additional problems that didn't exist before. From a purely human perspective, the problems our modern world faces make us feel sorry for those being born today—what currently unknown and unimagined problems will they face in their years on this earth?

As a parent, I am thankful that my children are past the growing up stage. I look at the young families and young children in my church and wonder what kind of a world they will find in the years ahead. There has never been a day in the history of the world when the ministry of encouragement is more needed than it is today. Of all the roles I play as a parent, the greatest role is to be a cheerleader. Children growing up in the calamitous culture we face today need all the love, support, encouragement, and cheering on that their parents can give. James Dobson, the champion of the family, has said that parents have one priority toward their adolescent children: "Just get them through it." And the way we get our children through the tough growing up years in today's world is through encouragement more than anything else.

Encouragement is the urgent priority of our day. I am so deeply committed to this concept that I believe a church that does not develop its skills as encouragers will soon phase out of any meaningful ministry in its community. There are so many discouraged people in today's society that encouragement—coming alongside those who are discouraged—is one of our most neglected avenues of ministry.

ENCOURAGEMENT IS THE UNIQUE PRIORITY OF OUR GOD

The second reason we need to study encouragement and become versed in its practice is that encouragement is uniquely characteristic of our triune God. Each member of the Godhead—God the Father, God the Son, God the Holy Spirit—makes encouragement a matter of priority. Paul uses the word *paraklesis*, encouragement, in 2 Corinthians 1:3 to describe God the Father, calling Him the "God of all comfort [encouragement]." In 2 Thessalonians 2:16, Paul describes Jesus Christ as the one who has "given us everlasting consolation [encouragement]." And the Holy Spirit is so identified with encouragement that it is one of His names. In John 14 and 16 the

Holy Spirit is called the *paraklete*—the Comforter (KJV), the Helper (NKJV, NASB), or the Counselor (NIV) (John 14:26). The Holy Spirit's ministry is to come alongside believers and lead them into all truth and to encourage them with the truth of God (John 16:13). When we come alongside people and do the same thing—encourage them on the basis of the truth of God—we are following in the ministry of the third person of the Trinity.

The Father encourages, the Son encourages, and the Spirit encourages. Anyone who is a believer should be an encourager as well.

ENCOURAGEMENT IS THE UNDERLYING PURPOSE OF OUR BIBLE

The third reason we need to learn how to be better encouragers is that it is the underlying testimony of the entire Bible.

In our age of market research, the church has learned how to attract a crowd and send them out full of warm fuzzies—pumped up and excited as if they have been to a pep rally. Now no one likes rallies more than I do. I can even give a pep talk when I need to. But what I have discovered—and what the Christian market researchers are discovering—is that if our pep talks are not based on the Word of God, the encouragement and enthusiasm they generate will not last. The resulting discouragement you feel when you come down off a temporary high is sometimes worse than the way you felt in the first place.

The steps to encouragement and fulfillment that are man-made will not last. But we have been given a Book by God which has truth in it that will encourage all who partake of it in a way that will last. Paul says, for instance, that the whole Old Testament was given as a source of encouragement for New Testament believers: "For whatever things were written before [the Old Testament] were written for our learning, that we through the patience and comfort [encouragement] of the Scriptures might have hope" (Romans 15:4). If we do not get our encouragement from the Word of God, it is not an eternal type of encouragement.

But the New Testament is filled with words of encouragement as well—especially in the Pastoral Epistles, those letters Paul wrote to Timothy, Titus, and Philemon. Paul the apostle was the mentor and teacher of these young men, instructing them in how to carry out the work of the ministry. Over and over in Paul's instructions to them he identifies the Word of God as a source of encouragement for them to use in the lives of those to whom they minister.

In 2 Timothy 4:2–3 we find the classic instruction by Paul to Timothy to preach the Word: "Preach the word! Be ready in season and out of season. Convince, rebuke, exhort [encourage], with all longsuffering and teaching. For the time will come when they will not endure sound doctrine." Paul says that the Word of God is to be used to convince, rebuke, and encourage (exhort), and it is to be done with longsuffering—doing it over and over again. And he says to do it by teaching. The primary task of pastors is to teach the Word of God in such a way that it encourages.

The teaching of God's Word brought encouragement in three distinct ways in Paul's letters to the Thessalonians. In chapter four of 1 Thessalonians, Paul is explaining to the believers why they shouldn't worry about those believers who have already died—whether or not they will go to heaven along with those who are alive when Christ returns. He spends most of the chapter teaching on this subject, and then in the last verse (18) says, "Therefore comfort [encourage] one another with these words." Paul's teaching on the future of those who have died in Christ was a great encouragement to the church.

In the fifth chapter, verses 1–10, Paul teaches on the Day of the Lord (verse 2). When he explains the doctrine of the Rapture of the church, he concludes with these words in verse 11: "Therefore comfort [encourage] each other and edify one another, just as you also are doing." Paul wants the truths he is teaching to be a source of mutual encouragement for the church.

Finally, in 2 Thessalonians 2, Paul concludes the doctrinal teaching he has given with his desire that Jesus Himself "comfort [encourage] your hearts" (verse 17). Throughout the rest of the New Testament there are many references to individuals whose claim to fame was that they encouraged others. We will meet many of them as we proceed through the subsequent lessons in this study on encouragement.

Someone has said that being encouraged is like working in the hot sun all day and then stopping to sit under a shade tree with a cool glass of lemonade. That's what it means to be encouraged. Paul identified the man Philemon as one who was an encourager— one who was a refresher of other people. In Philemon 1:7, Paul says, "For we have great joy and consolation [encouragement] in your love, because the hearts of the saints have been refreshed by you, brother." Wouldn't that be a great epitaph: "The hearts of the saints were refreshed by you, brother." As a pastor, that's what I want to do more than anything else through my teaching of the Word of God and the life I live—to refresh the hearts of the saints.

ENCOURAGEMENT IS THE UNCOMMON OPPORTUNITY TO BEGIN A NEVER-ENDING PROCESS

Encouragement is like throwing a pebble into the water and watching the ripples radiate out into infinity. Paul touches on this concept in 2 Corinthians 1:3–4 when he says that God comforts [encourages] us so that we can turn around and comfort another with the same comfort we have received from God. Properly done, encouragement begins with God and continues from one person to the next without end.

It's natural for it to happen that way. The most natural thing in the world for you to do when you are encouraged is to encourage someone else. And the opposite is true as well: When you are discouraged, you are likely to discourage people with whom you come in contact. It is so easy to pay no attention to little words of encouragement we offer, thinking that they are insignificant. But your word of encouragement to another may be the very thing that turns a person's day, or life, around.

A man whom I have admired for many years is Joseph Bayly, now at home with the Lord. One of his greatest contributions as a writer and editor was his books about suffering and dying. Rather than being focused on morbidity, he wrote his books on these subjects out of his own experience—Joseph Bayly had to bury three of his own sons during his lifetime. One of his sons died when only eighteen-days-old; one died at age five from leukemia; and the third died at age eighteen from hemophilia complications following a sledding accident. Joseph Bayly had more understanding about death, dying, and heaven while he was alive than anyone I know of.

When Joseph Bayly's eighteen-year-old son died, he was engaged to be married to a godly young woman. A few days after her beloved's death, the young woman paid a visit to Joseph Bayly and his wife. She gave them a copy of a poem that had meant a great deal to her, written by the German pastor Dietrich Bonhoeffer in 1945 just three months before he was executed by the Nazis. It was a poem that expressed Bonhoeffer's hope in God's unfailing goodness even in the face of suffering and death. Bonhoeffer himself was engaged to be married when he was executed, and the poem was delivered to his fiancée after his death. Here are two of the verses from Bonhoeffer's poem:

> Should it be ours to drain the cup of grieving
> Even to the dregs of passion at Thy command,
> We will not falter, thankfully receiving
> All that is given by Thy loving hand.
>
> While all the powers of Good aid and attend us,
> Boldly we will face the future, be what it may.
> At even and at morn God will befriend us,
> And, oh, most surely on each new year's day!

When Joseph Bayly wrote a book about heaven, he included the poem in his book. Thirty years after Bonhoeffer's death, and twelve years after the death of his eighteen-year-old son, Bayly received a letter from a pastor in Massachusetts. The pastor told of giving a copy of Bayly's book on heaven to a woman who was seriously ill in a Boston hospital. The woman stayed up all night in the hospital reading the book, such comfort it brought her in her own hour of suffering. Not long after reading Bayly's book, the woman, Maria Von Wiedermeier, died. She was the woman who was engaged to Dietrich Bonhoeffer when he had been executed by the Germans.

What a path Bonhoeffer's word of encouragement traveled! From Bonhoeffer, to his fiancée, to Bayly's son's fiancée, to Joseph Bayly and his wife, to a pastor, then back to Bonhoeffer's fiancée, Maria Von Wiedermeier in the last days of her life. We should take more seriously the words of Solomon in Ecclesiastes, "Cast your bread upon the waters, for you will find it after many days" (Ecclesiastes 11:1).

Dear friend, when you give away encouragement, you start a process that may never, ever end. You may never know what will happen with the word, the little written note, the putting of your arm around the grieving, hurting person. By your act of encouragement, you start a process that just keeps going on and on. I encourage you to be an encourager because it is so needed in the day in which we live, because it is characteristic of the ministry of God himself, because encouragement is the underlying message of all the Bible, and because it is an uncommon opportunity to start something that may never end. All believers ought to give themselves to the task of learning to be the best encouragers they can be.

1. Read Romans 15:1–7.

   a. Those who are strong are to do what with their strength? What are they not to do? (verse 1)

   b. How does verse 1 apply to encouragement within the life a believer?

   c. For whose good are we to please others? What does this lead to? (verse 2)

   d. Verse 3 tells us that Christ embodied giving unto others. List three specific examples from the life of Christ where this is displayed.

e. What was God's Word written for? (verse 4)

f. What two attributes found in Scripture are given in verse 4?

g. It is easy to see how Scripture is comforting, but how is Scripture patient? Explain.

h. What does Scripture produce in the life of the believer? (verse 4)

i. Paul's prayer is for believers to become what? According to Whom? (verse 5)

j. He reiterates this by saying we are to glorify God in what two ways? (verse 6)

k. Explain how praising God with one mind and voice correlates with the command to encourage one another.

l. Paul wraps it up with what final command? For what purpose are we to fulfill it? (verse 7)

2. Read 2 Corinthians 1:3–5.

a. God is the Father of _____ and the God of all _____. (verse 3)

b. When does God comfort us? For what purpose? (verse 4)

c. How does verse 4 put any suffering we might undergo in a new light and context?

d. Verse 5 says that the sufferings of Christ equate to consolation through Christ. Explain the significance of the words "of" and "through" in their context and how they are critical in properly understanding this verse.

3. Read 2 Thessalonians 2:16–17.

   a. What two marvelous things has God given us through Jesus? By what? (verse 16)

b. What does Paul say that God will do for His children? (verse 17)

c. How has the truth of verse 17 encouraged your heart? How can you share that with others today?

DID YOU KNOW?

Moses offers a sterling example of how we as believers should encourage one another no matter the personal circumstances we might be facing. Because of his disobedience to God (Deuteronomy 32:51), Moses was not allowed to enter the Promised Land. He easily could have sulked in despair that he was not able to lead Israel into that place. But instead, he gathered the people together and spoke these words of encouragement to the nation of Israel and his successor, Joshua: "Be strong and of good courage, do not fear nor be afraid of them; for the Lord your God, He is the One who goes with you. He will not leave you nor forsake you" (Deuteronomy 31:6).

A RESURRECTION OF HOPE

Luke 24:13–35

In this lesson we discover the ultimate reason for human hope and victory over discouragement.

OUTLINE

Born with a sunny disposition and a cheery outlook, some people rarely get discouraged. But not even optimism is a sufficient answer for the day of death that approaches every person. Only one truth is sufficient to remain encouraged even in the face of death.

   I.   **Act One: Discouragement**
      A. Doubt
      B. Disappointment
      C. Despair

  II.   **Act Two: Dialogue**

 III.   **Act Three: Discovery**

Following the crucifixion of Jesus, Jerusalem was reverberating with the aftershocks of that tumultuous event. Everyone was talking about what had happened; everyone had an opinion. Many thought that once Jesus was taken out of the picture, life would return to normal.

But for many, there was mourning and despair in their hearts. They had believed that Jesus was their Messiah, but not necessarily for spiritual reasons. They had hoped that the yoke of Roman oppression finally would be removed from their necks and they would be set free by the coming of the Messiah foretold by the prophets. But now, the One they thought might be the Messiah had been taken to a cross and hung until He was dead. His body had been sealed in a tomb; and, as far as they knew, that was the end of their hopes and dreams.

But then, on the first day of the week following the Friday of crucifixion, rumors began to circulate that Jesus' tomb had been found opened—and He was not inside! People reported seeing Him —ten instances in all, five of which occurred on one day.

Early on the first Easter Sunday (the first day of the week following the Jewish Sabbath), He appeared to Mary Magdalene; then later to the women who were returning to the tomb. Soon after, He appeared to ten disciples in the upper room, then to Peter privately. But on the afternoon of that first Easter Sunday, toward dusk, He appeared to two men who were making the journey from Jerusalem to Emmaus, a distance of about seven miles. These two had been followers of Jesus and had heard the reports of the Resurrection—but they didn't believe what they had heard. They were downcast and dejected. They had left their faith in Jerusalem and were returning to start life over again in Emmaus. As much as a geographical journey home, it was a spiritual journey as well— an attempt to reconcile the events of the last three days. But little did they know their lives were about to be changed by a "stranger" they met on the road to Emmaus.

The two disciples' encounter with Jesus on their way home is the most detailed record of His post-resurrection appearances. Rather than to Mary or any of the other disciples, this extended account is with two men about whom we have learned nothing. Cleopas (Luke 24:18) is mentioned the only time here, and the other disciple isn't even named. As during His earthly ministry, Jesus continued appearing and appealing to ordinary people with genuine needs even after His resurrection.

Verses 13 to 35 of Luke 24 are like a short, three-act play: The first and second acts take place on the road to Emmaus, Jesus' appearance changing the disciples' discouragement into a dialogue with himself. The third act takes place in Emmaus over a meal where the disciples' eyes are opened and their hearts filled with new hope and encouragement.

ACT ONE: DISCOURAGEMENT

There is no better word than discouragement to describe what Cleopas and his traveling companion were feeling. And yet discouragement is just the general description of three different levels of feelings that they—and we—feel when we are deeply discouraged. Discouragement moves from doubt or disbelief to disappointment, and even to despair.

Doubt

In Luke 24:10–11, we learn that when the apostles and followers of Jesus heard the initial news of His resurrection, they considered the reports "like idle tales, and they did not believe them." The two disciples traveling to Emmaus were among those who had been gathered with the larger group that had received the first reports of the Resurrection. They apparently agreed with the rest that the reports were just rumors, just wishful thinking. It is obvious from their actions that they didn't believe. Would they have left Jerusalem to return to Emmaus if they really believed Jesus was alive?

Disappointment

There is a thin line between doubt and disappointment, and these two disciples crossed it quickly. Verse 21 records their words— "we were hoping"—which reveals their shattered expectations.

Their expectations were indeed for liberation from Rome, but certainly for more than that. Jesus had been their friend, their leader in spiritual matters, and He was their hope for the future. The fulfillment of all the Old Testament prophecies was said to be part of His mission, which meant the promised return of God's blessing upon His chosen people. And now all these expectations had come crashing down to the ground and sealed in a tomb. Rumors notwithstanding, they believed Jesus was still there in the tomb, and they were filled with disappointment.

Despair

Doubt and disappointment, if unchecked, can lead quickly to despair—the loss of all hope. Perhaps these men had made serious lifestyle changes in order to follow Jesus. Perhaps they had put their reputations on the line with their families and neighbors. Now they were returning to face the embarrassment of having been wrong, to face the taunts of "I told you so" of those who had mocked their initial belief. Despair had overtaken these two disciples on the road back home.

ACT TWO: DIALOGUE

Suddenly, verse 15 states, Jesus "drew near" and joined them as they walked toward Emmaus. The language of the text indicates that Jesus was probably walking behind them and hastened His step in order to catch up and join them.

What takes place is almost humorous. Jesus is the center of the disciples' conversation, yet they didn't know it was Jesus himself who had just joined them as they walked. This happens to me on occasion since I travel so frequently; and sometimes you just want to blurt out, "That's me you're talking about!" That was the situation with the disciples and Jesus that day. Yet Jesus doesn't reveal who He is, but enters into their conversation so as to begin to transform the disciples' despair into hope and joy once again. Imagine having a personal dialogue with Jesus on the day of His resurrection!

Verses 19–24 reveal what the disciples believed about Jesus. They believed He was a prophet, and they had great confidence in His miracles and His teachings (verse 19). In verse 21 they express their belief that He was going to be the Redeemer of Israel. In spite of all they believed, they didn't believe the most important thing— that His death was a necessity and His resurrection a reality. As a result, their belief was inadequate. In spite of hearing the reports of the women who went to the grave, the words of the angels at the grave, and the testimony from the apostles, they still didn't believe Jesus was alive.

There is a theological lesson here for us: It is possible to be a Christian and not understand the Resurrection, but it is impossible to be a Christian without believing in the Resurrection. The resurrection of Jesus from the grave is the foundation of all the encouragement and comfort we need for life on this side of heaven. According to 1 Corinthians 15, we are still in our sins if Jesus did not come out of the grave alive. God raising Jesus from the dead, demonstrating power over death, is God's validation of the work that Jesus did in our place on the cross. If He is not alive, we are still dead in our sins.

So these disciples believed some, but not enough. At this point, Jesus enters their conversation and begins to dialogue with them. But rather than telling them what they needed to believe and revealing himself to them, He begins to draw out of them what they believe and are thinking. He presents a model for us to follow with those who don't believe. He opened the Scriptures to them (Luke 24:27) and began to patiently explain everything in the Old Testament concerning the Messiah. But not without a word of chiding. They, as His followers, should have known better, should have believed what the prophets had said (verse 25). If we knew the Old Testament better, we would know it is simply a portrait of the coming Messiah, Jesus Christ. The stories, the typology, the imagery—all of it points toward and finds its culmination in the person of Christ.

Jesus' dialogue with these two disciples was like a mini-Bible conference. Can you imagine sitting under the teaching of Jesus and hearing Him explain the entire sweep of Old Testament history? Did Jesus use Genesis 22 where Abraham takes his son Isaac to be sacrificed on Mount Moriah as a picture of His own sacrificial death? Did He turn to Isaiah 53 where the servant (Messiah) of God is pictured as a suffering servant, taking upon himself the punishment deserved by others? Or did He take them through Psalm 22 where numerous aspects of David's life are duplicated exactly in the crucifixion experience of Jesus on the cross?

When Jesus taught in the synagogue in Nazareth at the beginning of His ministry (Luke 4:16–22), He taught from the scroll of Isaiah. But they would not have had an Old Testament scroll as they walked along the road to Emmaus. Rather, Jesus just taught them from His heart knowledge of the Old Testament. The Word of God just flowed from His lips as He expounded on the plan of God for the salvation of Israel and the Gentiles as revealed in the Old Testament.

With every turn in the road, a new insight came from the Old Testament about the Messiah. The disciples must have been captivated by what they were hearing; and before they knew it, they had reached their destination. As they entered Emmaus, Jesus acted as if He were going to leave them and go farther (Luke 24:28). So taken were they with what they had learned on the road from this stranger that they persuaded Jesus to join them for the evening meal. They entered what was apparently one of their homes and sat down to share a meal together.

ACT THREE: DISCOVERY

When Jesus "took bread, blessed and broke it, and gave it to them" (verse 30), the eyes of the disciples were opened, and they suddenly recognized who Jesus was. Perhaps they had seen Jesus do this very thing numerous times in the preceding months and years. We don't know exactly how their eyes were opened, but we do know from verse 35 that it was in the act of His blessing and breaking the bread that their eyes were opened.

I have heard numerous sermons in my life comparing this event to the communion meal which we share together—that when we break bread together, our eyes are opened to see Jesus in wonderful new ways. That may be true, and it is a touching thought; but it has no basis in the text of this Scripture. This passage is certainly not talking about a parallel to communion, and it is not talking about something that will happen to or for all believers. It is talking about something that happened for those two disciples to whom Jesus was ministering that day in the village of Emmaus.

I am going to speculate a bit on what might have happened at the dinner table that caused the eyes of the disciples to be opened. See if you agree with my thinking. First of all, it was unusual for Jesus to come in and seemingly assume the role of the host in another person's home. That is, it is Jesus who picks up the bread, offers a blessing, and breaks it for the two disciples. If someone did that in our home, we would think they were being a bit presumptuous— and perhaps the disciples thought this stranger was a bit out of order as well.

But when Jesus broke the bread and handed a piece to Cleopas, then another piece to the other disciple, what did they probably notice for the first time? The stranger's nail-scarred hands. In a moment of wonder and insight, whoever noticed Jesus' hands first probably exclaimed to the other, "It's Him! It's Jesus!" The combination of hearing a blessing from Jesus they had probably heard before, Jesus role of leadership in breaking bread and offering a blessing to God, and the scars on His hands may have all come together in an instant and caused their eyes to be opened. And as soon as they recognized Him, He vanished from their sight. We don't know why or how— the text just says that He did.

Jesus probably left them in order for the impact of what they had just realized to have its full impact. Had he remained with them, they would have wanted to stay in Emmaus and continue to talk to Him and get more answers to their questions. But by leaving them, the thing we would expect occurred—they hit the Emmaus road once again. But this time, they were headed back to Jerusalem.

The transformation in the lives of these two men is beyond description. Just a few short hours before, they had traveled from doubt to disappointment to despair. Now, truth was once again burning in their hearts as a result of what Jesus had explained to them and of seeing Him alive (verse 32). The combination of knowing what was supposed to happen (based on the Old Testament) and the proof that it had happened (the resurrection of the Messiah) was exactly what they needed. The written and living Word of God transformed their lives.

Remember what time of day it is. They had just sat down to the evening meal, so it was near dark, the end of the day. They had just finished a two or three hour walk from Jerusalem. They were tired, dusty, and emotionally spent. Yet, as a result of an encounter with Jesus, and gaining new understanding of the purposes of God, they jump up and walk the seven miles back to Jerusalem that very night. They wanted to go back and add their report to the reports they had failed to believe earlier in the day—Jesus was alive! Just a half hour earlier, the thought of walking back to Jerusalem would have been impossible. Now, they fairly flew back to find the disciples. An encounter with the risen Lord Jesus Christ is the most encouraging thing that can happen to anyone.

For those disciples, the road from Jerusalem to Emmaus was the road that heightened their hope and destroyed their discouragement. When we find ourselves in the midst of discouragement, we need to get on a road that leads to an encounter with Jesus. Meeting Jesus through the Word, through the life of a fellow believer, through worship, or through prayer is the surest remedy for discouragement. If your heart is hurting within you because of despair, you need to encourage yourself in God's Word—hear from Jesus Christ. Discouragement and despair cannot exist in His presence.

APPLICATION

1. Read John 16:33.

   a. Why has Christ spoken and revealed Himself to us?

   b. What does the world offer us? What should be our response? Why?

2. Read 2 Corinthians 4:1–6.

   a. Why are we as believers not to lose heart in spite of our circumstances? (verse 1)

   b. List the three things that we as believers should not and do not partake in. (verse 2)

   c. How are we to openly commend ourselves to every man? (verse 2) Explain whatyou think that involves.

   d. What has blinded the perishing from the Gospel? (verse 4) Who is that?

   e. What are we to preach to the lost? What are we not to preach? (verse 5)

   f. What does verse 6 say is the light that shines in the darkness?

g. What are some ways that you can show someone that light of hope this week?

3. Read Ephesians 1:3–6.

   a. What have followers of Christ been blessed with? Where are they found? (verse 3)

   b. When did Christ choose us to be His own? (verse 4) What is your response to that stunning thought?

   c. Christ chose us that we might take on what two attributes? (verse 4)

   d. How did God choose us to be His own? (verse 5)

   e. Why did God choose us to be His own? (verse 6)

   f. How can the realities of verses 5–6 give you hope and encouragement in daily life?

4. Read 1 Thessalonians 5:5–11.

   a. We are described as being what two things? What are we not part of? (verse 5)

   b. What are we instructed to do in verse 6?

c. What things happen in the nighttime? (verse 7)

d. What two acts does being sober involve? (verse 8) Why do you think those of the day are to arm themselves?

e. What are Christ followers appointed to? What are we not appointed to? (verse 9)

f. When do we live together with Christ? (verse 10) Why is that so encouraging?

g. Because we are girded with the armor of God and are sons of light, what are we commanded to do?

DID YOU KNOW?

We are only given the name ("Cleopas") of one of the two men who walked with Jesus on the road to Emmaus. The other remains anonymous. Although there is great importance in a name, throughout the Bible we see God made Himself known to nameless people. The nameless shepherds were on the outcast of society, yet God chose to allow them to observe the greatest birth in history (Luke 2:20). Also, Jesus revealed His deity to the nameless Samaritan woman sitting by the well in John 4:1–26. God has always been consistent in seeking out those on the periphery of life. As Jesus said in Matthew 5:3, "Blessed are the poor in spirit, for theirs is the kingdom of heaven."

WHEN ALL ELSE FAILS

1 Samuel 30:16

In this lesson we learn that it is possible to encourage ourselves in the Lord.

OUTLINE

The Bible says we can do all things through Christ who strengthens us. Does that include self-encouragement? Or does it take another person to encourage us "in the Lord"? There are at least three spiritual disciplines that, when practiced, result in encouragement.

I.   **Encouraging Ourselves Through Solitude**

II. **Encouraging Ourselves Through Scripture**

III. **Encouraging Ourselves Through Song**

S omeday, someplace, somehow . . . you will find yourself
   discouraged and alone—at the same time. As we saw in our last
   lesson, sometimes it helps to have a fellow believer alongside
you when discouragement hits. But that is not always the case. You
may be on a business trip, stuck in an unfamiliar airport. You may
be confined to a hospital bed in a different city. Or you may be in
your own home, up late at night, facing a major crisis in your life.
How do you battle discouragement "when all else fails" and there
is no one there to encourage you to go on.

The solution is a biblical one—you learn to encourage yourself.
It is biblical because we find that one of our Old Testament heroes,
David, encouraged himself during a dark period in his own life. His
story is found in 1 Samuel 30, and it recounts part of the period of
David's life when he was being persecuted by King Saul. When
David killed the Philistine giant, Goliath, he became the toast of Israel.
Everyone in Israel praised David's courage and valor—everyone
except one person, that is. King Saul was consumed by jealousy and
set out to destroy David.

David lived in the wilderness for a period, running and hiding
from Saul and his soldiers. He became the leader of a ragtag bunch
of 400 soldiers who were in debt, were distressed, and discontented
with life (1 Samuel 22:2). To escape Saul on one occasion, David
and his men crossed over the Israelite border into Philistia to hide.
The Philistines almost made David and his men go to war with them
against David's own people, the Israelites. They decided against that
strategy and allowed David and his men to return to Ziklag where
their families and possessions had been left. But when they arrived
at Ziklag, they discovered the Amalekites had invaded and burned
Ziklag and kidnapped their wives and children. His own men were
so upset at David for allowing this to happen that they threatened
to stone him (1 Samuel 30:6a).

In modern terminology, we might say David was having a bad
day. He had 400 ruffians about to stone him, several hundred missing
women and children (including his own wives), and a bounty on his
own head from the king of Israel. Though he was surrounded by
people, David was completely alone in his agony. There was not one
person there to encourage him or support him. Yet David took it upon
himself not to give in to his circumstances. So David "strengthened
himself in the Lord his God" (1 Samuel 30:6b).

I know a little bit of what David must have felt like, as do most pastors. Because pastors spend so much of their time encouraging others who are discouraged, they sometimes have little strength in reserve for themselves. And often there is no one for them to turn to for encouragement—someone who understands the pressures of the ministry. I am blessed to have men to whom I can turn for strength and encouragement in my walk with the Lord, but it has not always been so. Whether we are a pastor or a parent or a public citizen, there are going to be times when we are facing the pressures of life alone.

The key to surviving those times is to remember that God has given us everything we need for righteousness, godliness, and victory in our lives. Though we are to bear one another's burdens, we are also to learn to bear our own when we find ourselves alone. The resources God has given are more than sufficient for encouraging and strengthening ourselves in the Lord.

Having spent quite a bit of time studying the life of David, I want to suggest to you three things that I believe David could have done in order to gain perspective when his world came crashing down upon him at Ziklag. He could have encouraged himself through solitude, through Scripture, and through song.

ENCOURAGING OURSELVES THROUGH SOLITUDE

Solitude, or silence, is almost an unknown concept in today's world. In fact, most people are very uncomfortable with silence—they have to have a radio or television or something playing in the background when they find themselves alone. Yet it is not difficult to find examples of biblical characters who isolated themselves in order to gain encouragement and direction from God.

Elijah was such a man. After facing King Ahab, God sequestered him by the Brook Cherith and dealt with him in isolation. Then after he went to Mount Carmel and had a great victory over the prophets of Baal, he got depressed and ran away. But God put him in a cave on Mount Horeb and dealt with him there until he could hear the still small voice of God. God often seems to have built isolation into the lives of people He wanted to use.

In the noisy culture we live in today, we must learn to isolate ourselves—figure out how to be alone with God. I have always loved the story of Susannah Wesley, the mother of nineteen children, two of whom were John and Charles Wesley. The only way she could be alone for a moment with God during her busy day was to sit down and pull her apron up over her head in order to talk to God. Most of us don't have to go to that extreme to find a place of solitude; but if we need to, we should. I believe David was the kind of person who was committed to the practice of solitude—being alone with God. His psalms are filled with references which reflect the amount of time he spent thinking God's thoughts after Him during lonely nights as a shepherd.

Psalm 46:10 says, "Be still, and know that I am God." In Psalm 62 David wrote these words: "Truly my soul silently waits for God; from Him comes my salvation. He only is my rock and my salvation" (verses 1–2a). The prophet Isaiah put it this way in Isaiah 30:15: "In quietness and confidence shall be your strength." Anyone who thinks his time is so valuable that he cannot find time to be quiet and be alone will eventually not be valuable to anyone but himself. In order to have anything to give to other people, we must first receive from God.

The purpose of solitude is to talk with God and to let God talk with you. And the place of solitude is anywhere you can find that provides an opportunity for quiet reflection and communication with God. Jesus withdrew to two places primarily: the mountains and the seashore. I have access to both where I live, and I avail myself of the opportunity to draw apart to either place on a regular basis.

I was interested to learn from the life of Billy Graham that it was in a place of solitude that he made a commitment to God that was a turning point in his life. In his early years, a friend of Graham's came under the influence of liberal theologians and began to try to sway Graham away from a position of trust in the inerrancy and authority of Scripture. While staying in a cottage in the woods, he resolved to make a decision about this matter. He went into the forest to pray and came back to the cottage to read his Bible some more. Then, in the middle of the night, he went back into the forest again. Finding a tree stump about the height of a pulpit, he placed his Bible there and got down on his knees and poured out his heart to the Lord. He committed himself from that point on never to doubt the authority of the Word of God, but to preach it faithfully for the rest of his life.

In a moment of quietness and solitude, Billy Graham made a life-changing decision that has resulted in the salvation of thousands of people around the world. While the issues may be different, the practice should be the same. Meeting God in a place of quietness and solitude is a step any believer can take in the process of encouraging himself.

ENCOURAGING OURSELVES THROUGH SCRIPTURE

The second way any believer can encourage himself is through the Word of God. David was familiar with the promises of God as recorded in the five books of Moses (the only Scripture he would have had at that time). His psalms are filled with references to the covenant promises made to Israel and delivered through Moses. David lived on the basis of those promises and used them to bolster his flagging faith.

Romans 15:4, which we have referred to already in our studies, is a perfect example of how the Word of God can serve to build the faith and hope of the New Testament believer. Paul says, "For whatever things were written before were written for our learning, that we through the patience and comfort of the Scriptures might have hope." As you recall, the word "comfort" is the same Greek word that means "encouragement." Encouragement and strength are to be gained through the reading and study of God's Word. Once encouragement is received, hope is renewed.

When Paul wrote Romans, the New Testament as we have it was not complete. He was obviously referring to the books of the Old Testament as the source of encouragement. And nowhere is that encouragement found in greater abundance than in the Psalms

- Psalm 27:1 "The Lord is my light and my salvation; whom shall I fear?"
- Psalm 34:4–9a "I sought the Lord, and He heard me, and delivered me from all my fears. They looked to Him and were radiant, and their faces were not ashamed. This poor man cried out, and the Lord heard him, and saved him out of all his troubles. The angel of the Lord encamps all around those who fear Him, and delivers them. Oh, taste and see that the Lord is good; blessed is the man who trusts in Him! Oh, fear the Lord, you His saints!"
- Psalm 43:5 "Why are you cast down, O my soul? And why are you disquieted within me? Hope in God; for I shall yet praise Him, the help of my countenance and my God."

- Psalm 46:1–2, 10–11 "God is our refuge and strength, a very present help in trouble. Therefore we will not fear, even though the earth be removed, and though the mountains be carried into the midst of the sea. Be still, and know that I am God; I will be exalted among the nations, I will be exalted in the earth! The Lord of hosts is with us; the God of Jacob is our refuge."

When you are discouraged, the best friend you have apart from your personal prayer relationship with God is the Scriptures. I'm not saying don't buy Christian books, but I offer this word of warning: We have gotten to the point in the church culture where we would almost prefer to read a book about the Bible rather than the Bible itself. If a book has anything worthwhile to say, it will be based on the truth of God that is in the Bible. If we want to encourage ourselves, the very first place we ought to go is to the pages of God's Word.

ENCOURAGING OURSELVES THROUGH SONG

The last way that I believe we can learn from David to encourage ourselves is through song—the offerings of praise to the Lord through music and song. I believe, apart from Scripture and a personal relationship with the Lord, music is the most blessed of the gifts God has given to us.

There is one song in the Old Testament Scriptures that few believers have ever read because it is tucked away in the little book of Habakkuk. It is a song born out of discouragement. Habakkuk had been called by God to minister during a time of great wickedness in Israel. Habakkuk wanted God to judge Israel for her sin, but was shocked to learn that God was going to use an even more wicked people, the Chaldeans, as His means of judgment. He was totally discouraged by God's actions because He didn't understand at all what God was doing.

But when we get to the end of Habakkuk's prophecy, we find a hymn of faith that Habakkuk wrote in the midst of his discouragement:

"Though the fig tree may not blossom, nor fruit be on the vines; though the labor of the olive may fail, and the fields yield no food; though the flock may be cut off from the fold, and there be no herd in the stalls—yet I will rejoice in the Lord, I will joy in the God of my salvation" (Habakkuk 3:17–18).

Habakkuk was saying, "In spite of what I don't understand about the circumstances, I will nevertheless rejoice in the Lord." He encouraged himself by singing a song of praise to the God whose actions he didn't understand, but whom he was willing to trust anyway. The Hebrew words Habakkuk uses in this hymn would cause some raised eyebrows in some of our churches—but such is Habakkuk's desire to praise his God in song. The first Hebrew verb of verse 18 literally says, "I will jump for joy in the Lord." And the second verb he uses says, "I will spin around to the God of my salvation." Habakkuk was in the moment of his deepest discouragement, yet used music to bring himself up out of it. He was ready to jump and spin around for joy because of who God is!

God has used music over and over in my own life to minister to me, to encourage me in difficult times. As examples, I'll mention three songs in particular that God has used in my life through the years. The first is one I rely on often because it has to do with God's faithfulness even when we are unfaithful. Whenever I have failed to be as faithful as I want to be, "Great Is Thy Faithfulness" is a hymn that will get my eyes off of my failures and onto God's character.

Then there are times in my life when it seems everything is going in the opposite direction of where it should be going. Horatio Spafford's great hymn, "It Is Well With My Soul," written in a time of great personal calamity in his family, always straightens out my thinking in times when circumstances have gone awry. Finally, Andraé Crouch's great song, "Through It All," came to me at a time when my wife was critically ill in the hospital. I played that song on a cassette countless times in my car during those difficult days.

The next time you are discouraged and alone, take the three steps you have learned in this lesson to encourage yourself: Get alone, get in the Word, and get a song of praise on your lips.

APPLICATION

1. Read Psalm 19:7–11.

    a. God's law is _____. What does it do? (verse 7)

    b. His testimony is _____. What does it do? (verse 7)

    c. The Lord's statutes are _____. What do they do? (verse 8)

    d. The Lord's commandment is _____. What does it do? (verse 8)

    e. Look over the adjectives and descriptions you have written about the power of God's Word. What have you learned about Scripture through these verses?

    f. How are God's judgments described in verse 9? Why then should we fear His judgment?

    g. Recall and describe a time when God's Word was sweet to you like honey.

    h. What are two tangible, daily benefits of adhering to Scripture? (verse 11)

2. Read Psalm 27:6.

   a. What is David's response to deliverance?

   b. List some ways (in addition to singing) that you can offer "sacrifices of joy" to the Lord for His goodness.

3. Read Psalm 119:25–28.

   a. How low is the psalmist at the point of verse 25? What is his prescription for revival?

   b. What does he ask God to do in verse 26? Why don't we pray like that more often in times of duress? Explain.

   c. In order to understand God's Word fully, what must we do? (verse 27)

   d. What alone can strengthen the soul? (verse 28)

   e. Describe some of the foolish ways in which we try to strengthen our souls apart from the Word of God.

4. Read Psalm 119:49–56.

   a. List all the ways in which God's Word has impacted the psalmist in verses 49–50.

b. Verses 51 and 53 describe the plight of the psalmist. What is going on?

c. What is his response to all of this? (verse 52)

d. Explain how verse 54 embodies all three points found in this chapter's study.

e. What does the psalmist do in his dark hour? (verse 55)

5. What is the common underlying theme found in all of the Psalms we've examined?

DID YOU KNOW?

There are numerous accounts in Scripture where singing preceded a great and marvelous intervention by God for His people. In the Old Testament, the Moabites and the Ammonites—enemies of God, hopelessly surrounded Judah and the people of Jerusalem. But 2 Chronicles 20:22 tells us that, "…when they began to sing and to praise, the LORD set ambushes against the people of Ammon, Moab, and Mount Seir, who had come against Judah; and they were defeated." And in Acts 16:25, Paul and Silas were "praying and singing hymns to God" right before the Lord delivered them from their prison cell by means of a great earthquake.

FRIEND THERAPY

Selected Scriptures

*In this lesson we learn how to be a
channel of encouragement to others.*

OUTLINE

High-powered electric lines criss-cross our country. They do
not produce electrical power, they merely receive it on one end
and dispense it on the other. Likewise, we can be conduits of
encouragement. As we are encouraged, so we can encourage others.

I. **Encouraged by What I Sense**

II. **Encouraged by What I Hear**

III. **Encouraged by What I Read**

IV. **Encouraged by What I Feel**

The wonderful Broadway production, *My Fair Lady*, contains a memorable line that sets the stage for our study in this lesson. The English professor Henry Higgins has entered into a wager with Colonel Pickering. He proposes that he can transform Eliza Doolittle, a Cockney flower girl, into a young woman of charm and grace such that she can pass for a member of an aristocratic European family. Higgins works with her manners, her bearing—and especially her speech—until Eliza's transformation is complete. Returning home from a glittering event where Eliza passes her test with flying colors, the pompous Higgins relaxes in his easy chair and asks Eliza to bring him his slippers.

Eliza has had it. She explodes with indignation, having reached her limit in being treated as a cultural experiment rather than a person. She howls at the professor, reverting to her native Cockney speech, and declares, "I will not be passed over!"

Her words are the words of many a person in today's world, though they often go unsaid. No one likes to be passed over; and yet many people, even in the body of Christ, feel as if they are alone, not known by anyone. We are so busy with our lives that it is easy to sit next to someone and hardly even know they are there. Someone has suggested that many Americans suffer from "attention deprivation"—we just don't know whether anyone really cares about us or not.

The Scriptures are filled with admonitions and instructions to God's people which, if followed, would keep anyone in the church of Jesus Christ from ever feeling that way. And they are not instructions to pastors or church staff. They are instructions to every member of the body of Christ. It is the members of Christ's body who are responsible for encouraging and building up every other member. We are to instruct, teach, admonish, stimulate, build up, pray for, carry the burdens of, confess our sins to, submit to, help, and encourage one another. In fact, all of those verbs could fall under the category of encouraging and building up one another.

A great passage in the Old Testament on this subject is Ecclesiastes 4:9–12:

> Two are better than one because they have a good reward for their labor. For if they fall, one will lift up his companion. But woe to him who is alone when he falls, for he has no one to help him up. Again, if two lie down together, they

will keep warm; but how can one be warm alone? Though one may be overpowered by another, two can withstand him. And a threefold cord is not quickly broken.

This passage clearly speaks to the power of community. God did not create us to live and function alone, but with the help and support of one another. Four kinds of encouragement are found in this key passage:

1. We can help one another. Two are better than one because there is a reward for their labor. When you are faced with a difficult task and someone comes along and says, "Why don't you let me give you a hand with that," we feel encouraged—and the task goes more than twice as fast. Our church experienced this repeatedly when we were building our worship center. The more people who came and joined in, the quicker the work went and the better we all felt. There is something wonderful about living and working in community with others.

2. We can stimulate one another. Two people lying together will keep each other warm on a cold night. And while we don't experience that literally that often in our heated homes, the concept is still valid. By living our lives next to others, we stimulate each other in all kinds of ways. All of us get cold toward the things of God at times—it's our fallen human nature to do so. Nothing warms us up afresh like the presence of others who are on fire for the Lord. Just as hot embers in a fireplace serve to keep the other embers glowing when they are next to each other, the same is true of people in the Lord.

3. We can protect one another. Though one may be overpowered, two can withstand. Scripture says that the devil is like a roaring lion seeking someone to devour. Just as animals draw close to one another when lions are on the prowl, so believers can defend themselves from the devil by not straying away from the body of Christ—becoming a spiritual straggler and fair game for the devil. We need accountability which provides mutual protection and defense against the temptations and dangers of this world.

4. Finally, we can encourage one another. If we fall, our companions can lift us up; but woe to him who falls alone, for he has no one to lift him up. It is a dangerous and scary thing to fall, whether spiritually or physically, and suddenly realize there is no one around to pick you up and get you back on your feet.

I sometimes take my trail-bike motorcycle up into the California mountains to ride the rough terrain and enjoy the beauty of God's creation. On one occasion, I had ridden off the trails farther and farther until I began to lose my sense of direction and get an uneasy feeling about my ability to find my way back. In the rough terrain, I took a spill on my bike and thought I was unhurt until I noticed blood pouring down my leg. Suddenly it hit me—I was lost and bleeding seriously. For just a moment, I felt that sense of panic and fear that I know many people feel emotionally all the time: I'm all alone and no one knows that I'm lost and hurting.

Fortunately, I found my way out of the mountains and recovered from my injury—but too many people don't. They have no one who knows where they are, to pick them up when they fall, and guide them to safety.

Fifteen passages in the New Testament talk about the "one-another" ministries we are to have to each other, and five of them have to do with encouragement:

- 1 Thessalonians 4:18. "Therefore comfort [encourage] one another with these words."

- 1 Thessalonians 5:11. "Therefore comfort [encourage] each other and edify one another."

- 1 Thessalonians 5:14. "Now we exhort you, brethren, . . . comfort [encourage] the fainthearted, uphold the weak, be patient with all."

- Hebrews 3:13. "But exhort [encourage] one another daily."

- Hebrews 10:25. "Not forsaking the assembling of ourselves together . . . but exhorting [encouraging] one another."

Five times in Thessalonians and in Hebrews we are instructed to have the ministry of encouragement to one another. But how do we actually receive encouragement from another person? By talking for a moment about the ways we receive encouragement, we can learn how to give encouragement to others.

ENCOURAGED BY WHAT I SENSE

Encouragement is something you can sense from another person. A great example of someone who didn't sense encouragement was Job. When his three "friends" came to visit him in his affliction, all they did was point out to him that he must have sinned. There was no encouragement, only condemnation.

But a good example of someone being totally focused on another person is the story of Mary, the sister of Martha. When Jesus came to visit them at their house, Martha couldn't tear herself away from the kitchen long enough to focus attention on Jesus. But Mary—she never left Jesus' presence! She was focused on only one thing, and that was being near the Lord. That must have been incredibly encouraging to Jesus, to see someone as devoted as Mary was to seeking the best. In fact, Jesus said that it was Mary who did the better thing by staying focused on Him (Luke 10:42).

Do you know what it is like to have people focus their attention on you? Have you ever been the object of focused attention? You know that person is there for you, that they care about you, that they are not worried about any of the other things that are going on. You know in your heart when somebody has your best as their objective. You can sense when their attention is focused on you and you alone.

I am encouraged when I know people care about me, not because of what I do, not because of who I am, not because of where I live, just because they care about me. If I can sense that from other people, then it tells me that is the way I can encourage others as well.

ENCOURAGED BY WHAT I HEAR

The old saying, "Nobody cares how much you know until they know how much you care," applies here. Sometimes we open our mouths before we have opened our hearts, and people can tell the difference. We earn the right to speak to others by focusing our attention on them as persons first. A Japanese proverb says, "One kind word can warm up three winter months."

The Book of Proverbs seems to be the central source in the Bible for the wise use of words in personal relationships. For instance, Proverbs 12:25 says, "Anxiety in the heart of man causes depression, but a good word makes it glad." Once when I was experiencing a time of deep discouragement in the ministry (and experiencing what is true about pastors, that they are the only people in the church without a pastor), I got a call from another pastor in the same city. He was a friend of mine who called me up just to tell me that he knew I was going through a difficult time, and to let me know he loved me and was praying for me. He said he was there if I needed him for anything, and then prayed with me on the phone. Every week for a period of time after that he called with a word of encouragement. Since then, and motivated by his example, I have had the opportunity to return the ministry of encouragement to him, pastor to pastor.

This pastor-friend called at just the right time with just the right word to encourage me in a difficult hour. He poured courage into my heart, dispelling the fear I was wrestling with about my circumstances. He focused his attention on me for several weeks and spoke words of encouragement to me. Because I was greatly encouraged by the words I heard from him, I have learned to encourage others by similar thoughtful words.

ENCOURAGED BY WHAT I READ

In generations gone by, writing was the way everyone communicated. Before telephones, and now abbreviated email messages, people wrote out their thoughts to one another in longhand. Some of our greatest insights into history and biography come from the collections of letters preserved by those who received them.

Today, there is a great need for a revival of the art of writing words of encouragement to one another. Whenever I receive a note, card, or letter from someone, it is such an encouragement to me. I can hold it in my hand, see the person's handwriting, save it to read again, and even keep it for years as a token of my friendship with that person. Even a short note of a few sentences can literally turn a person's day, or life, around.

In our church, we have even taken time on Sunday mornings to furnish every person with a note card and envelope, and asked them to write a personal note of encouragement to someone whom they know. They address the envelopes, and we stamp them and mail them from the church. We are trying to encourage people to be encouragers through what they write—so others can be encouraged through what they read.

Even when you don't get an immediate response or acknowledgement from someone you've written to, be assured you have probably encouraged them. I remember once when my son was extremely disappointed with how he had played in a high school basketball game. The next day, I wrote him a long letter of encouragement and had my secretary deliver it to his school. I expected that night to receive great words of appreciation from my son for the letter I wrote him—but he said nothing. Then, several months later, as a "P.S." on my Father's Day card, he included this small note: "Thanks for the note of encouragement." He had received my letter, and been encouraged by it, which is all that matters.

Encouraged by What I Feel

We are encouraged by what we sense, what we hear, and what we read from others who take time to show an interest in our lives. And finally, we are encouraged by what we feel from others. By that, I mean the encouragement that comes through the physical act of touching. I realize this is a sensitive area because there certainly can be inappropriate forms of touching. But I am talking here about those appropriate moments when a hug, an arm around a shoulder, or a gentle squeeze of a hand can communicate encouragement to the discouraged.

Jesus could have healed people in any number of different ways. But often, He incorporated the human act of touching. He reached out and touched the leper (Matthew 8:3), touched Peter's mother-in-law (Matthew 8:15), touched the ears and tongue of a deaf man who had a speech impediment (Mark 7:33), and touched the ear of the high priest's servant (Luke 22:51). Paul did the same thing in his ministry, reaching out and laying his hands on the father of Publius who was ill, healing him (Acts 28:8).

Many people today are not comfortable touching or being touched. We have put on such veneers of dignity and respectability that we suggest to others we don't need such a familiar experience as a hug or a touch. But we do. As doctors tell us, the skin is the largest organ in the body, and it is one of the five ways we receive communication. Yet we have all these hundreds of square inches of skin, and the sensory receivers are going to waste because we don't get touched as much as we should!

I'll never forget a wonderful evening spent with a fellow pastor in another state. Before parting to go our separate ways, he wrapped his long arms around me and hugged me tightly, telling me how much he loved me and of his renewed desire to pray for our ministry. Even today, I think I can feel the imprints of his arms and hands on my back. He communicated his love to me with a powerful bear hug that made an indelible impression on my heart and mind.

I feel encouraged by what I sense, hear, read, and feel. And because I am encouraged that way, I know others will be encouraged by my focused attention, my words, my notes, and my touch.

1. Read Proverbs 12:25–26.

    a. What can anxiety cause? (verse 25) Have you found this to be true in your own life? Explain why or why not.

    b. What is the remedy for anxiety and depression? (verse 25)

    c. List some simple ways to offer a good word to someone.

    d. Why is it doubly important to find good friends? (verse 26)

2. Read Proverbs 27:6, 9–10.

    a. Explain how and why the wounds of a friend are faithful?

    b. The good counsel of a friend is likened to what? (verse 9)

    c. Put into your own words the explicit advice offered in verse 10.

    d. Are you the kind of friend whose counsel leaves others uplifted like perfume? If not, what can you do about it? And if so, what can you work on to be an even better friend?

3. Read John 15:13–15.

   a. What is the greatest act of love there is? (verse 13) Who exemplified this?

   b. How can we be called friend of the One who gave His life for us? (verse 14)

   c. Why is Christ able to call us friends? (verse 15) Why does that carry with it such an enormous weight of responsibility?

4. Read Hebrews 10:19–25.

   a. Why are we able to enter the Holiest? How are we to enter it? (verse 19)

b. The veil that separated God and man has been replaced by what? (verse 20)

c. List the verbs describing our actions to be taken in verse 22. What is the common thread here?

d. Why should we not waver in our faith? (verse 23)

e. In considering one another, we are to do what two things? (verse 24) Why is this an appropriate response and action to take in light of verses 19–23?

f. We are to exhort one another even more so as what approaches? (verse 25)

g. How does verse 25 especially relate to us as believers and the church today?

DID YOU KNOW?

There are wonderful examples of friendship found throughout the Bible. David and Jonathan were great friends who loved each other as their own soul (1 Samuel 18:1–4.) And even though Ruth was Naomi's daughter-in-law, they displayed a love and a friendship that goes beyond family lines (Ruth 1:16–17). Even Jesus had an inner circle of friends that He was closer to out of the twelve disciples. Peter, James, and John were the disciples Jesus often took with Him during extraordinary times in His life. They were the only three men to witness many events, like the Transfiguration (Matthew 17: 1–3).

MR. ENCOURAGEMENT

Acts 11:24

*In this lesson we will meet a man who was nicknamed
"Son of Encouragement."*

OUTLINE

We know what a "son of a gun" is—a real character with an "explosive"
personality! But what about a "son of encouragement"? We find one
in the book of Acts named Barnabas—a man who was characterized
by his comfort and benevolence toward all.

I. **Encouragers Perform While Others Pretend**

II. **Encouragers See Potential Where Others Only See Problems**

III. **Encouragers Care More About People Than Programs**

I took a speech class in college because a girl named Donna Thompson was taking the class (her last name is now the same as mine). While she was an excellent student, I mostly goofed-off in that class. One day, the professor took me aside after the class and said, "You know, I don't know what others have told you about your abilities, but I believe you have real potential. I believe in you. You ought not to mess around in class. If you apply yourself, you might become a preacher one day."

I shrugged off his advice—but I didn't forget it. In fact, I remember that moment as if it were yesterday. Rarely do we forget the moments when someone speaks an encouraging word to us that impacts our life.

Just as that professor had a lasting and encouraging impact on my life, in this lesson we will meet a man in the New Testament who had that kind of impact on many people's lives—so much so that I like to call him Mr. Encouragement. His name was Barnabas, a name that actually means Son of Encouragement. The record of his activities is spread throughout the book of Acts, but he is best described in Acts 11:24: "He was a good man, full of the Holy Spirit and of faith."

"Good" was not an offhand word as we might use it today. It meant that he was a virtuous man, generous, kind, and full of good works. He was good in the sense that God is good. And his goodness proceeded from his being full of the Holy Spirit—meaning he was controlled by the Holy Spirit. He was a man whose faith and works were evenly evident in his life.

Acts, chapter four, is where Barnabas is first mentioned. His name was originally Joses, but he was given the name Barnabas by the apostles (Acts 4:36). And it is not difficult to see why he came by that name. He was from Cyprus, a Mediterranean island off the coast of Syria, just north of the Holy Land. He makes his entrance into the unfolding story of the church at a very critical time.

The church was born at Pentecost (Acts 2) and began to multiply rapidly. There was no formal structure such as we have today— boards, committees, and so forth. The apostles were in charge of the church and all of its activities. In order to meet the needs of those who had come to Christ, especially the poor who had no means of support, many people contributed what they could; and the apostles dispersed it to meet the needs of the people.

Barnabas, from the wealthy island of Cyprus, owned property which he sold for the purpose of helping to meet the needs of the infant church in Jerusalem. He sold the property and "brought the money and laid it at the apostles' feet" (Acts 4:37). It is Barnabas's actions which lead us to our first point about encouragers.

ENCOURAGERS PERFORM WHILE OTHERS PRETEND

Barnabas was the genuine article. He didn't hesitate to take what he owned and sell it for the purpose of meeting the needs of others. There was no pretense about Barnabas—he just did what he observed needed to be done. But Barnabas's actions take on added significance when viewed in the context of the next chapter of Acts.

When the word got out about what Barnabas had done, two other people in the church decided they would like to get some of the same acclaim as Barnabas did. So Ananias and Sapphira sold a piece of property just like Barnabas had done; but instead of giving all the money to the apostles, they kept part of it for themselves. The problem was not that they didn't give it all to God. No one had asked them to give anything. The problem was that they said they were giving it all to God. It was their deceit that got them in trouble. You know the story as told in Acts, chapter five. The Lord judged them by taking their lives for the lies they had told to the apostles.

That story illustrates the difference between performers and pretenders. Barnabas was a performer, while Ananias and Sapphira were pretenders. Encouragers perform while others pretend. All of us have found ourselves thinking, "I really need to call so-and-so and see how they are doing," or "I really need to go visit that person and offer to help them." We think about doing something, but we never do. Encouragers think about doing it and then do it! They don't pretend to be encouragers, they are encouragers.

Encouragers are active people. Often you wonder how they even knew about the needs of another person. They are always listening and picking up on things in conversation, making mental notes about how they can help. Then quietly, without fanfare, they find a way to meet the needs they have heard about. I thank God for the encouragers in the body of Christ, those who are constantly performing, putting their faith into action. Like Barnabas, they are good people.

If we look behind the scenes in Acts, we discover that Barnabas was one of the most influential people in shaping church history.

Why? Because of his impact on the apostle Paul. Acts, chapter nine, tells the story of Paul's conversion to Christ on the road to Damascus. Paul had been a zealous persecutor of Christians before his conversion; and after his conversion, he became just as zealous—only now he was zealous for the Gospel. That often happens. Energetic opponents of the Gospel become energetic advocates of the Gospel when they are saved. Their hard-driving style stays the same, but for a new cause. And that's exactly how Paul was.

The problem was that everyone in Jerusalem was still afraid of him (Acts 9:26). The disciples there didn't really believe he had been converted. They probably thought he was just trying to infiltrate the church. But Barnabas came alongside Paul, listened to his story, and decided to vouch for him (Acts 9:27). So the church in Jerusalem received Paul into the fold. How would church history have been impacted if Barnabas, Mr. Encouragement, had not been there to put his arm around Paul and say, "He's okay. He's one of us"?

ENCOURAGERS SEE POTENTIAL WHERE OTHERS SEE ONLY PROBLEMS

This leads us to the second principle about encouragers: They see potential where others see problems. Just as the church in Jerusalem saw Paul as a problem, Barnabas recognized his great potential. While some will say, "I'm not so sure," encouragers will say, "Let's give it a try."

Barnabas proved himself an encourager in this regard in another instance recorded in Acts 15. Interestingly, it also involved Paul whom Barnabas had stood beside previously in Jerusalem. Here is the setting: Paul had been out on a missionary journey and established a number of churches in Asia Minor. He decided it was time to go back and pay those churches a visit to check on their progress (Acts 15:36). Barnabas had been Paul's companion on the first journey; and when it came time to leave on the second journey, Barnabas wanted to take along a young disciple named John Mark. He had accompanied Paul and Barnabas on their first journey, but had deserted them along the way (Acts 13:13; 15:38). We don't know why John Mark left and returned home, but this did not sit well with the apostle Paul at all.

When Barnabas wanted to take John Mark along on the second journey, Paul would have none of it. Paul was so goal oriented that anyone who quit before the goal was reached was not to be trusted again. Paul saw a problem with John Mark, but Barnabas saw potential. Paul saw a quitter, but Barnabas saw a young man who needed a second chance. So sharp was the disagreement between Paul and Barnabas that they split up and went their separate ways. Barnabas took John Mark and sailed for Cyprus while Paul took Silas and left for Asia Minor.

We could call this a doubling of the missionary effort, but in reality it was a disagreement, plain and simple. Yet by the end of Paul's ministry, writing in the fourth chapter of 2 Timothy, Paul comments on how valuable John Mark had been to him. In fact, Paul asked Timothy to bring Mark with him when he came (2 Timothy 4:11).

The most interesting thing about this event is this: Who had Barnabas put his arm around back in the early days of the church in Jerusalem? Paul. When no one would have anything to do with Paul because of his prior reputation, Barnabas stood beside him. In the current situation, Barnabas, still being the encourager, tries to get Paul to do for John Mark what Barnabas had done for Paul. But Paul wasn't willing to compromise at that point in his life and ministry. He had not yet become the encourager that he seems to have become by the end of his ministry.

When we are encouraged by another person, we need to remember the benefit it brought to us. Chances are good that we will be given an identical opportunity down the road to do the same for another person. Because we were once a problem, and someone saw the potential in us, we need to be on the lookout for the potential in others.

Because our church is involved in a number of schools of our own—preschool, grade school, high school, and college—and we have many public school teachers in our church, I am well aware of the process that takes place between teachers in the school setting. Everyone knows that teachers will get together and discuss the students who are moving up from one grade to the next. "Watch out for this one," they'll say, or, "She will be one of your best students." Labels get attached to students—usually unintentionally—by teachers. So when a teacher sees a "problem student" come into the classroom at the beginning of the year, they see problems instead of potential.

How blessed is the teacher who can receive the reports that are sometimes necessary to pass on, but still look for the potential in every student. How blessed was I, a goof-off in speech class, when a college professor pulled me aside and spoke to me about my potential. And how blessed is the person at any place in life who, in spite of past failures and problems, is viewed in terms of his potential. It takes an encourager like Barnabas to see people that way. Will they sometimes disappoint you? Yes, but make them have to climb over your encouragement and possibility perspective in order to mess up. Don't encourage their future failures by agreeing that they are a problem person.

ENCOURAGERS CARE MORE ABOUT PEOPLE THAN PROGRAMS

Finally, encouragers care more about people than they do about programs. Now don't get me wrong—programs are important. Someone has to manage the church facilities and the money and the Sunday school teachers and on and on. Those are all valid roles in the church. But even those people who are involved in programs have to learn to be encouragers, to see that programs are only there for the purpose of building up and strengthening people.

There is an illustration of this principle in the life of Barnabas in the eleventh chapter of Acts. This was the setting: In the early days of the church, the Gospel was preached only among the Jews though God intended it for non-Jews as well. But the Gospel message made its way to Antioch, and there a number of Greeks believed in Jesus—"the hand of the Lord was with them, and a great number believed and turned to the Lord" (Acts 11:21). When the leaders of the church in Jerusalem heard this news, they sent Barnabas to Antioch to investigate. When Barnabas got to Antioch and saw what the grace of God was accomplishing, "he was glad, and encouraged them all that with purpose of heart they should continue with the Lord" (Acts 11:23). We would expect nothing less from Mr. Encouragement. It was as if no one had explained the program to Barnabas that only Jews were to receive the Gospel. He rejoiced that Greeks as well as Jews were turning to Jesus!

The most amazing thing about Barnabas was that he left immediately and went to Tarsus to get Paul to help him teach the new converts. For a whole year, Paul and Barnabas met with the church in Antioch and "taught a great many people" (Acts 11:26). Barnabas wasn't into competition. He wasn't hesitant at all to bring Paul into the revival at Antioch and share the responsibility and excitement with him. In fact, if you notice in roughly the first half of the book of Acts, the two men are usually referred to as "Barnabas and Saul (or Paul)." It appears that Barnabas was truly a mentor to Paul in the early years of his spiritual growth. Then as Paul's stature and influence grew, they began to be referred to as "Paul and Barnabas," which likely made no difference to Barnabas at all. He was much more interested in people and ministry than in programs and protocol.

Structure means nothing to encouragers. All they want to do is find somebody who's got a need and reach out and help them. How much we need people like that in the church today! We have more people willing to take care of structures than we do people who are interested in taking care of people. We stand in great need of more Mr. and Ms. Encouragers in the body of Christ—people who don't need a title, an office, a staff, a budget, a business card, a classroom. All they need is a chance to get next to a person who needs encouraging.

One of the greatest modern day examples of a Barnabas was Bob Pierce, the man who started World Vision, the great evangelical humanitarian aid organization that ministers to the needs of needy people around the world. While dying of leukemia, Bob Pierce took all his pain medication and traveled to Indonesia to visit one last time with a dear friend who was a missionary there. They encountered a young woman who was dying of cancer, but had no medication and was in terrible pain. She couldn't sleep at all, so severe was her pain. Because she had only a few days to live, Bob Pierce gave her all of his pain medication and instructed the missionary to make sure she took it until she died. They were ten days from the nearest place where he could get his own prescription refilled, yet he was willing to endure his own terrible pain for that time so that the young woman could die in peace.

Bob Pierce was a Mr. Encouragement; he had the heart of Barnabas. May their tribe increase in our day, that the discouraged in our world may be strengthened and given new hope.

1. Read 2 Corinthians 7:13–16.

   a. Why was Titus so joyful? (verse 13)

   b. Why does Paul not apologize for boasting in Titus? (verse 14)

   c. How was Titus received by the church? How has the recollection of this affected him? (verse 15)

   d. What is Paul's response to their treatment of Titus? (verse 16)

   e. Do we as a church receive each other in this way? If so, how? If not, why not?

2. Read Ephesians 4:7–16.

   a. Verses 7 and 8 tells us that we were each given what things? By Whom?

   b. Why was it crucial that Christ not only descended but also ascended? (verse 10)

   c. List all the different roles Christ has appointed for His followers to take. (verse 11)

   d. What are the two purposes for all those roles listed in verse 11? (verse 12)

   e. What is the end goal for all of us who call ourselves followers of Christ? (verse 13)

f. What are the things that we are to avoid partaking in? (verse 14)

g. How are we to interact with one another at all times? Why? (verse 15)

h. What builds up the body of Christ? (verse 16)

i. How can you apply this passage to your personal relationships, especially those with other believers?

3. Read Ephesians 4:25 –32.

a. Why does lying grieve the Holy Spirit? (verses 25, 30)

b. Give a specific example of how it is possible to demonstrate verse 26a.

c. Why do you think it is important to not sleep on anger?

d. What is the antidote given for those who steal? (verse 28)

e. What should not come out of our mouths? What should? Why? (verse 29)

f. What has the Holy Spirit done for each believer? (verse 30)

g. List all of the things of the flesh we are to abstain from. (verse 31)

h. How are we to act instead? Who is the greatest example of this? (verse 32)

DID YOU KNOW?

Although Barnabas isn't as well known as Peter and Paul in establishing the church, he served a valuable role in edifying the leaders of the early church. Behind every great hero in the Bible lies a person who encouraged him or her in the Lord. Mordecai was a great source of comfort and strength to Esther as she put herself in peril to save the Jews. Aaron spoke on behalf of his brother Moses before Pharaoh to bring forth the Exodus. And Elisha assisted Elijah in ministry for many years until he succeeded him and became a great prophet as well.

THE ENCOURAGEMENT ZONE

Selected Scriptures

In this lesson we learn how to build a strong marriage by the power of encouragement.

OUTLINE

As every husband and wife knows, marriage is life's most fulfilling and most challenging relationship. Courage can slip away through the years, leaving spouses discouraged. To stay encouraged, three things are needed: responsibility, intimacy, and transparency.

I. **A Renewed Commitment to Responsibility in Marriage**

II. **A Renewed Commitment to Intimacy in Marriage**

III. **A Renewed Commitment to Transparency in Marriage**

I have read the biographies and stories of many men and women who have left their mark on history. By the time I get to the end of the story of a person's life, it is amazing how apparent their values and priorities become.

For instance, I read the story of the famous magazine publisher, Malcolm Forbes. He was the man who coined the phrase, "He who dies with the most toys wins." And he lived his life in pursuit of that prize. He lived in the fast lane of the jet set, counting the rich and famous all over the world as his friends. He spent millions on lavish parties and exquisite baubles, all in pursuit of finding meaning in life. Yet it was apparent that, as he grew near the end of his life, he wondered about the value of his pursuits. After visiting the magnificent tombs of the Egyptian kings, he asked an associate, "Do you think I'll be remembered after I die?"

Another man, Admiral Richard Byrd, came much closer to encountering death face-to-face. Isolated for months in Antarctica in an 11'x 15' ice hut, he endured the ravages of loneliness, sickness from the fumes of his gasoline stove, and temperatures that reached 72 degrees below zero. Because he thought he was going to die before he was rescued, he spent a great deal of time evaluating his life's priorities and values. He came to the conclusion that, when all is said and done, the affection and understanding of one's family were the only two things that really mattered in life.

Two men, two differing world views. One committed to accumulating toys and good times before he died, the other reaffirming the proposition that relationships with the ones you love are the most valuable possessions on earth. The latter is certainly the more biblical perspective. Outside of one's relationship to the Lord Jesus Christ, nothing is more important than encouraging and strengthening the relationship of the family. And the heart of the family unit is, of course, the marriage relationship.

When God designed marriage, He created it to be an institution of oneness. No other relationship on earth is so designed as an "encouragement zone" as is marriage. Because of the oneness married couples share, continual opportunities for encouragement exist. And because of the intense and close proximity oneness creates, encouragement is an absolute necessity. Marriages cannot exist without mutual encouragement on a daily basis.

The record of the establishment of marriage is found in Genesis 2. Everything God created in Genesis 1 was "good," God said, except for the single state of the man. So God created for the man a counterpart—a woman. The Hebrew word for man is *ish*, and the word for woman is *ishah*. The woman was taken from the side of the man, fashioned from his rib (Genesis 2:21–22). The woman was not made from the ground, but taken from Adam so that Adam was incomplete until the woman was returned to him. Ish could not be complete without his Ishah.

St. Augustine, the great church father, put it this way: "If God had meant woman to rule over man, He would have taken her from his head. Had he designed her to be his slave, from his feet. But God took woman out of man's side, for He made her to be a help meet and equal to him." When God presented Eve to Adam, he said, "This is now bone of my bones and flesh of my flesh" (Genesis 2:23). He recognized that what was part of him had been returned to him.

There is an old Jewish rabbinical writing on this passage that fascinates me. It goes like this: "The man is restless while he is missing the rib that was taken out of his side, and the woman is restless until she gets under man's arm, from whence she was taken. It is humbling for the woman to know she was created for the man, but it is to her glory to know that she alone can complete him. Likewise, it is humbling to the man to know that he is incomplete without the woman, but it is to his glory to know that the woman was created for him."

In Genesis 2:18–25 we have the record of the beginning of the institution of marriage. But in verses 24–25 we discover three principles that are foundational to making marriage the encouragement zone God intended it to be, and which it must be if it is to reach its God-intended potential.

A RENEWED COMMITMENT TO RESPONSIBILITY IN MARRIAGE

Right from the start, in verse 24, are the most fundamental words about marriage ever spoken or recorded: "A man shall leave his father and mother." There probably is not a man alive who will not identify in some way with what I experienced in the hours prior to my own wedding. I did not have doubts about the woman I had asked to marry me. In no way did I think I had made a mistake in deciding to get married. But I confess that I was suddenly afraid.

All of a sudden (I remember this like it was yesterday) the truth hit me: "This is a great responsibility. I am asking someone to come and be a part of me. We are going to live together. We are committed to being together for the rest of our lives. This is a whole new chapter in my life. This is AWESOME."

Another frightening experience men usually have is when the first child is born. You realize that you are adding to your life the responsibility for a whole new person who is totally dependent on you for everything it needs—and will be for years to come. If you are a parent reading this book, I imagine you are silently remembering and affirming those awesome feelings that I am talking about. Fear, wonder, excitement—but mostly the awesome sense of responsibility that comes with marriage and beginning a family.

Unfortunately, what happens in marriage is that the sense of responsibility seems to diminish over time. It is evident from the statistics we read that most people begin marriage with a healthy sense of responsibility. But at the first sign of trouble, they somehow decide they aren't responsible—and often walk away from their commitment. We speak of "tying the knot" in marriage, and it is not a bad metaphor. A knot symbolizes something that holds things together when pressure is brought to bear. It's like the humorist who said that mountain climbers tie themselves together to keep the sane ones from going home! But in far too many cases, a knot that was tied firmly on the day of the wedding vows is being untied by one or both partners in the marriage. We have lost the sense of responsibility to keep our marriages together.

Dr. Robertson McQuilken, past president of Columbia Bible College (now Columbia International University), resigned his position in order to care for his wife who suffered from the advanced stages of Alzheimer's disease. In his resignation letter, he illustrated what responsibility to marriage vows should be about for every married person:

"My dear wife, Muriel, has been in failing mental health for about eight years. So far, I have been able to carry her ever-growing needs and my leadership responsibilities at the college, but recently it has become apparent that Muriel is contented most of the time that she is with me and almost none of the time when I am away from her. It is not just discontent. She is filled with fear, even terror that she has lost me, and she goes in search of me whenever I leave home. Then she may be full of anger when she cannot get to me. So it is clear to me that she needs me now full time. Perhaps it would help you to understand my decision if I shared with you what I shared at the time of the announcement of my resignation in the students' chapel. The decision was made, in a way, 42 years ago when I promised to care for Muriel in sickness and in health, 'til death do us part. So, as I told the students and faculty, as a man of my word, integrity has something to do with it, but so does fairness. She has cared for me fully and sacrificially all these years. If I cared for her for the next 40 years, I would not be out of debt yet. Duty, however, can be grim and stoic. But there is more. I love Muriel. She is a delight to me—her childlike dependence and confidence in me, her warm love, her occasional flashes of the wit that I used to relish, her happy spirit and tough resilience in the face of her continually distressing frustration. I do not have to care for her, I get to care for her. It is a high honor to care for so wonderful a person to whom I made a lifetime commitment 42 years ago."[1]

That is responsibility in marriage. That kind of commitment must be maintained and encouraged by both husbands and wives if marriages are to remain together. From an earthly perspective, having the most toys at the end of life is not the goal; having a committed and responsible marriage and family relationship is.

A RENEWED COMMITMENT TO INTIMACY IN MARRIAGE

The next thing God said about the marriage institution follows in verse 24. Not only is a man to leave his father and mother; he is to be "joined to his wife, and they shall become one flesh." "Joined," or "cleave" in the old King James Version, is literally the word "glue." A man is to be glued to his wife. The implications of this bonding are that it is to be permanent. Where there were two individuals, now there is one couple.

Everyone likes to focus on the physical aspect of intimacy in marriage, and of course it is important. But that is a small part of what total intimacy in marriage is all about. It is just the icing on the cake. Without encouraging spiritual and emotional intimacy first, physical intimacy will never reach its maximum fulfillment. Being joined together in marriage means being joined first spiritually, then emotionally, then physically. Spiritual intimacy is begun during the dating, or courtship, phase. If spiritual intimacy is not discovered and developed there, the relationship should go no further. God clearly says believers are not to marry unbelievers (2 Corinthians 6:14–18).

If spirit to spirit intimacy is found, then soul to soul intimacy can be developed. This is closeness at the emotional level, the level of personality and friendship. Finally, physical intimacy can be enjoyed upon the profession of marriage vows. When two people have become intimate spiritually and emotionally, they have the right to share physical intimacy, but not before. In the world, the process has been reversed, and far too many Christian young people are being influenced in the wrong direction. They are becoming intimate physically, then emotionally, then finally (if at all) spiritually. I want to tell you, my friend, that's backwards! And that is a large part of the reason for the marital mess our nation, and the church, is in today.

When people get married without having developed spiritual and emotional intimacy first, they end up living with someone whom they don't really know. I recall seeing a television news program about a man who had four different wives in four different parts of the country. He would visit each of them long enough to keep up pretenses, then leave for a "business trip" and go to visit another wife. That's an example of living with someone with whom there was no real intimacy. How could any of those "wives" not have known that something was amiss in this man's life?

When you know and are known in marriage on the basis of spiritual and emotional intimacy, that can be the most encouraging experience in the world. You love and are loved spiritually on an unconditional basis—which means you can love and be loved in spite of anything else (personality, physical attributes, and the like). What could be more encouraging? It's when we get God's priorities in "joining" out of order that our marriages become discouraging—and ultimately fall apart.

A RENEWED COMMITMENT TO TRANSPARENCY IN MARRIAGE

Finally, the third thing we learn about making marriage the encouragement zone it was intended to be is found in verse 25: "And they were both naked, the man and his wife, and were not ashamed." Adam and Eve had nothing to hide from each other, and this means far more than just physically. The focus here is about emotional, psychological, and spiritual transparency. They had completely clear consciences before one another and made no efforts to protect themselves or hide themselves from each other because of sin. When sin entered their lives, of course, this was changed.

Most partners in marriage would confess a desire to reveal themselves completely to their spouse, not to hide anything from the one they love. But they would also confess a fear of being known as they truly are. The blemishes, the sins, the wrong thoughts and desires—all of the baggage we carry with us is just too heavy and sensitive to open up before another person. Yet the strange thing is that most spouses wish their partner would do just that— yet they are afraid to say so and to reveal who they are as well. So both know what would be best, but both are afraid to venture into the uncharted and vulnerable realm of transparency. The fear of not being loved once their spouse discovers who they really are is too threatening, so they live pretending to be someone different.

I recall talking with a young man who had found his way to a church where I spoke as a result of hearing a radio advertisement. He wasn't a Christian and, at age thirty-three he had made and lost a million dollars three times—and was on the verge of losing his wife. He wanted to know how he could know if God was real. He was a junior version of Malcolm Forbes—trying to find what was real in life. I shared the Gospel and everything else I could in our brief time together to let him know that his life could have meaning and his marriage could be saved. He was learning what Admiral Byrd discovered—that marriage and family are everything.

Is your marriage an encouragement zone? Begin making it one today by recommitting yourself to responsibility, intimacy, and transparency with your spouse. That is the time-tested and God-honored way to make your marriage the source of encouragement God intended it to be.

Note:

1. R. Kent Hughes, *Disciplines of a Godly Man* (Wheaton: Crossway Books, 1991), 35–36.

1. Read Proverbs 17:9.

   a. Give a modern euphemism for the phrase "covers a transgression."

   b. Give a modern euphemism for the phrase "repeats a matter."

   c. Putting your modern euphemisms in place of those terms, does this truth still ring loud and true today? Why or why not?

2. Read Proverbs 17:17.

   a. Why does adversity weed out all but the truest friends?

3. Read Ephesians 5:1–7.

   a. What are we commanded to do? In what manner? (verse 1)

b. Why is the image of following like a child used in verse 1? What does that connotate?

c. How are we to simply live our lives? (verse 2)

d. How did Christ love us? (verse 2) How can we imitate that behavior with those around us?

e. List all of the things not fitting for believers in Christ. (verses 3–4) Are there things on the list that you need to work on?

f. What is the one behavior befitting a saint? (verse 4)

g. What is the consequence of exhibiting the traits on that list? (verse 5)

h. What is the result of the actions listed in verses 3–4? (verse 6)

i. What is Paul's blunt conclusion to these truths? (verse 7)

j. How does this passage underscore the importance of choosing friends and companions wisely?

4. Read Ephesians 5:22–28.

   a. What are wives to do? In what way? (verse 22)

   b. What are the two examples given of how a husband is to lead his wife? (verse 23)

   c. Why does this humbling and daunting responsibility get so taken out of context?

   d. Explain why the submission called for in verse 24 is so beautiful and fulfilling.

e. How are husbands to love their wives? (verse 25)

f. Verses 26–27 show how much Christ loved the church and what he did for her. What kind of actions and attitudes would a husband need to display to mirror that kind of love?

g. What is Paul's final and clear council for husbands to follow?

DID YOU KNOW?

Some men in the Bible stand alone when they are remembered; for instance, Moses, Joseph, David, and Paul need no qualifiers or addendums to be understood. But some men of the Bible cannot be properly referenced without naming their wives. It is hard to mention Abraham without Sarah or Joseph without Mary. These couples and their stories are so linked that referencing one without the other just doesn't quite seem proper or accurate. And this is also true of couples like Adam and Eve and Samson and Delilah, whose mutual sins bind them and mark and define their time together.

CHILDREN NEED CHEERLEADERS

Selected Scriptures

In this lesson we discover how to motivate children by using four kinds of encouragement.

OUTLINE

On a bad day, a parent might be heard to say, "These children are incorrigible!" What is actually true is that all children are "encouragable!"—that is, able to be encouraged. The challenge for parents and teachers is to learn encouragement skills that really work.

  I.   **Encourage Your Children With Focused Attention**

 II.   **Encourage Your Children With Individual Affirmation**

III.   **Encourage Your Children With Genuine Appreciation**

IV.   **Encourage Your Children With Physical Affection**

A young father loaded his two kids into their car seats and drove to the nearby hospital where his wife was on duty as a surgical nurse. Their mission was to deliver Mother's Day presents to their wife and mom. As they loaded back into the car to head home, the dad set the infant carrier containing his three month old son on the roof of the car while he strapped his older son in his car seat. Then the unthinkable happened—he got in the car and drove out of the parking deck with his youngest son still sitting in his carrier on the roof of the car!

He made it all the way onto an expressway before he heard the sound of something scraping on the roof of the car. Just as he realized what he had done, he saw the infant carrier slide down the back window, across the trunk, and disappear out of sight onto the expressway—into the path of oncoming traffic.

I'll tell you what happened later in this lesson. But for the moment, I want you to think of that little boy as a picture of where so many of our children are today. Growing up in the middle of a dangerous cultural expressway, totally unprotected, facing certain destruction by oncoming forces of evil. And no one seems to care. The national statistics on the state of young people in America today are frightening. But we don't even need to hear the statistics. All we have to do is look around us—on television, in movies, in our neighborhoods, perhaps even in our own homes—to know that children and teenagers are facing the most frightening present and future that any generation of American young people has ever faced.

Violence against and victimization of young people is increasing at an alarming rate. Parents are increasingly leaving children to function on their own. Homes where both parents are working are by default allowing children more and more unsupervised time, resulting not only in behavioral problems but emotional problems as well. Children are growing up insecure and disconnected from the support structure that the family is supposed to be.

And Christians are not immune. We may think that Christians who go to church every Sunday and try to do the right thing are not touched by these trends. But we are. And somehow the evils of the culture always have a way of spilling over into the church. It's time that Christians realize that good families don't just happen by accident. If there is any one thing I would say to parents, it's that we desperately need to learn how to be cheerleaders for our children. They need all the encouragement we can give them.

There are four ways we need to encourage our children in a day when they so desperately need it.

ENCOURAGE YOUR CHILDREN WITH FOCUSED ATTENTION

Opinions about the problems in our society affecting children are everywhere. But I believe the number one problem that harms our children is something you rarely read about: nothing. I'm not trying to be confusing here, but I want you to see that the problem is the absence of something that we should be doing. The "nothing" that I'm talking about is no focused attention. We are allowing a whole generation of young people to grow up without their parents giving them the focused attention they deserve and need. For the most part today, homes with both parents working just focus on logistics—who needs to get where at what time with what band instrument or sports equipment. All of our time and effort is focused on the things children do instead of on the children themselves.

Here is a letter written to his parents by a young boy who ran away from home. It painfully paints the picture I am trying to give you concerning focused attention:

"Dear Folks, Thank you for everything, but I'm going to Chicago and try to start some kind of new life for myself. You ask me why I did those things that got me in trouble, why I gave you so much static while I was at home. The answer is easy for me to give you. But I don't know if you'll understand. Remember when I was about six or seven years old and I used to want you just to listen to me? I remember all the nice things you gave me for Christmas and my birthday, and I was really happy with those things for about a week. . . . But the rest of the time during the year all I wanted was you. I just wanted you to listen to me like I was somebody who felt things. Because I remember when I was young, I felt things. But you always were busy. You never seemed to have time. Mom, you're a wonderful cook and you always have everything so clean, and you were tired from doing all those things that made you busy. But you know something, Mom? I would have liked crackers and peanut butter just as well if you'd only sat down with me a while during the day and said to me, 'Tell me all about it. Maybe I can help you understand.' I think that all the kids who are doing so many things that grown-ups are tearing out their hair worrying about are really looking for somebody that will have time to listen a few minutes, and who will really treat them as they would a grownup who might be useful to them, you know. Well, if anybody asks you where I am, just tell them I've gone looking for somebody with time 'cause I've got a lot of things I want to talk about.

Love to you all, Your Son."[1]

I don't know the young man who wrote this, but my heart aches for him and for thousands more like him who have gone into the dangerous expressways of life looking for someone who will focus just a little attention on them. Unfortunately, the people who focus attention on them out in the world too often don't have their best interests at heart. And that's where the statistics come from.

I'm always amazed by the stories about the remarkable Susannah Wesley—the mother of nineteen children that included John and Charles Wesley. Though only 10 of her children survived to adulthood, she still had a house full of young ones for the better part of twenty years. And the ones who reached adulthood did so admirably. Susannah Wesley used to devote one night a week to each of her children in their young years, just to focus attention on them. In a letter to his mother as an adult, John Wesley wrote, "Oh, Mother, what I'd give for a Thursday evening!" What was he saying? He was recalling the precious time he had alone with his mother one night a week, a time when she focused attention on him.

The first place we need to begin as a way of encouraging our children, a way of rescuing them from the dangers bearing down on them, is to give them our focused attention.

ENCOURAGE YOUR CHILDREN WITH INDIVIDUAL AFFIRMATION

The second way to encourage our children is by affirming their uniqueness and individuality. Helping children become content and satisfied with who God created them to be will go a long way toward keeping them from seeking ways to become someone they are not—and shouldn't try to be.

Proverbs 22:6 is a classic verse in this regard. While many interpreters take the "long view" of this verse—that it refers primarily to the future and the fact that children will come around when they are adults if we teach them correctly when they are young—I incline toward a different perspective. I believe the greater wisdom in this verse is to be found in the perspective of training each individual child in the way he or she should go—that is, according to their unique "bent" and personality. This is the essence of affirming each child individually in a way that speaks to them. This, of course, requires study and insight on the part of parents. One father I know keeps a notebook on his children, recording his observations about each one. It helps him separate them and resist the temptation to treat them all the same.

Too often in families we use one word to describe our progeny: "Kids!" We just lump them all together and refer to them en masse, as a single entity. Nothing could be farther from the truth. Each one is uniquely made in the sight of God, and it is the parents' job to discover who each of their children is and affirm them individually. Some are athletic, some aren't. Some are musical, some aren't. Some are outgoing, some aren't. Some are intellectual, some aren't. And if we don't know which are which, we'll frustrate all of them all the time.

My friend Tom Bissett authored a book in which he said that all children can be put under one of two labels: anti-authority kids or pro-authority kids. He cites Dr. Ross Campbell who says that the ratio is 3:1, anti-authority kids to pro-authority kids. That means the vast majority of kids are just naturally wired to resist authority. And yet, with spiritual matters, parents try to cram Christianity down the throats of all their children in such a way that it creates more rebellion than religion.

The solution to this is again found in Proverbs 22:6. The word "train up" in Hebrew comes from a root word that refers to placing a sweet substance on the palate of a newborn's mouth so as to stimulate their sucking reflex and encourage them to start nursing as soon as possible. When we train up children, we have to create a hunger in them, individually, for the things of God and for wisdom. We have to give them situations and advice in life that cause them to want to grow spiritually and know God. Children who accept spiritual truth because they are stimulated to pursue it themselves are more likely to keep it than those who have it forced on them whether they understand it or not. I talk to many adults, especially baby boomers, who are coming back to church after spending many years away from it. They got turned off by having religion forced on them as young people, but now they are hungry and seeking it out themselves.

We need to know our kids and learn how we can best minister to their needs. Individual affirmation is tremendously encouraging to a young person.

ENCOURAGE YOUR CHILDREN WITH GENUINE APPRECIATION

The third way to encourage our children is with genuine appreciation for who they are. Children who live in a world run by adults often get the impression that they are second-class citizens. Just because they are not yet adults does not mean they should not be respected and esteemed for who they are—especially during the critical years when their perceptions of themselves are forming.

In Colossians 3:21, Paul gives a word of instruction that is critical at this juncture: "Fathers, do not provoke your children, lest they become discouraged." It is so easy to raise our children by pointing out to them only the things that they are doing wrong. For the word "provoke" in this verse, the NIV translation says don't "embitter" your children; don't make them bitter. Nothing will make a child more bitter, and therefore cause him to become deeply discouraged, than to constantly hear only the things he has done wrong. If the only attention a child gets is the attention that comes from doing something wrong, a child will become bitter, or provoked.

Ken Blanchard, the author of *The One Minute Manager*, wrote another book called *The One Minute Father*. While not a Christian book, it is filled with insights consistent with biblical childrearing. One of the ones I like the most is the idea of walking around trying to catch your kids doing something right. We usually do just the opposite, don't we? Instead of looking for what they're doing wrong, look for what they're doing right and express appreciation for it. Some parents actually believe their kids never do anything right. That's obviously not true—it's just that they aren't looking for the right things. Rich DeVos, cofounder of one of America's great business success stories, says the most important management skill he ever learned was how to be a cheerleader.

That is a great skill for parents to learn as well: How to be a cheerleader for your kids. The greatest coaches are not the ones who yell the loudest, but the ones who know how to motivate their players by affirming their strengths and appreciating every contribution they make, no matter how small. That's the kind of coaches parents need to be for their children. Regardless of their contribution to the family team, each child needs to be appreciated for who they are and the contribution they are making.

ENCOURAGE YOUR CHILDREN WITH PHYSICAL AFFECTION

Finally, I need just to touch on physical affection. I put that last in the list because, to be honest, it's impossible for a parent who gives their child attention, affirmation, and appreciation not to give them lots of physical affection also. I know this may come more naturally for some moms and dads than for others. But physical affection—the hugs and kisses, wrestling on the floor, sitting in the lap, and holding when the tears flow—is going to come more and more naturally for the parent whose heart is in the right place in the first three areas.

Physically expressing our appreciation to our children is a wonderful way for them to learn that physically, they are attractive and "okay." In a culture that increasingly measures esteem and acceptability on the basis of physical appearance and attractiveness, parents getting close to their kids physically is just another way to say, "I'm comfortable being around you just the way you are. I enjoy being close to you and welcome the times we can hug or sit close together to read a book or watch a movie." Even as teens, our kids need to know that physical affection is a normal way of saying, "I love you." The best way to raise an encouraged, affectionate child is to be an encouraging, affectionate parent.

Since I know you're wondering . . . miraculously, the infant carrier hit the pavement and skidded upright until it stopped in the expressway. The person following their car slammed on his brakes, turned his car sideways in the lane to protect the child, and held it until the father was able to back up and retrieve his son. You and I need to be that person for our children—acting as a shield for them so they don't get run over by the dangers hurtling toward them in life.

Attention, affirmation, appreciation, and affection—four ways you can keep your kids encouraged.

Note:

1. Robert Raines, *Creative Brooding* (NY: MacMillan Co., 1966), 81–82.

1. Read Proverbs 20:7.

    a. If a man walks in integrity, what is the result upon his children?

    b. What does this say about the role of a parent's faith in the life of a child?

2. Read Proverbs 20:11.

    a. What does the proverb reveal about children and a sense of conscience?

    b. How can and should this proverb affect the way a parent trains and raises a child?

3. Read Matthew 7:9–12.

   a. What point does Jesus establish with his two examples in
      verses 9–10?

   b. What keeps us from acting upon the startling truth that Jesus
      presents in verse 11?

   c. What is the Law described in verse 12?

   d. How can that Law relate to how we raise our children? To how
      we treat our friends?

4. Read Luke 18:15–17.

   a. How did the disciples strongly react to the presentation of children to Jesus? (verse 15) Why do you think they acted this way?

   b. What does Jesus link children with in both verses 16 and 17?

   c. What do you think Jesus means when he says we can only enter the kingdom like little children?

   d. List some of the qualities of children that are endearing and precious.

e. Do you edify and encourage these traits in the children you interact with? If so, how? If not, how can you begin to do that?

f. How can you be more childlike and Christ-like in your faith? In your relationships?

5. Read 2 Timothy 3:14–15.

a. What is vital that we continue to do in our walk? (verse 14)

b. What should be said of the children that we are able to influence in our lives? (verse 15)

c. Why is it so important to remember what we already know, especially in regard to our faith?

d. How can this truth be applied to our interaction with children?

DID YOU KNOW?

Most believers know the great commandment given in Deuteronomy 6:5 – "You shall love the Lord your God with all your heart, with all your soul, and with all your strength." But the instructions tied to that commandment are often ignored and lost in its teaching. In reference to that great commandment, Deuteronomy 6:7 admonishes that, "You shall teach them diligently to your children, and shall talk of them when you sit in your house, when you walk by the way, when you lie down, and when you rise up." We are clearly instructed to not only live out this commandment, but to teach it to our children as well!

THE WRITE WAY TO ENCOURAGE

Selected Scriptures

In this lesson we learn five benefits of extending encouragement through writing.

OUTLINE

It's been said that, "If it's not in writing, it doesn't exist!" Speaking an encouraging word means someone has to remember what was said, and by whom. Encouragement in writing becomes a permanent record that can be a blessing many times over.

   I.   **Written Encouragement Is Deliberate**

  II.   **Written Encouragement Is Definite**

 III.   **Written Encouragement Is Direct**

 IV.   **Written Encouragement Is Durable**

  V.   **Written Encouragement Is Distance-Proof**

God meant the church of Jesus Christ to be a living organism that builds up and encourages each person who is a member of it. And words are one of the most powerful ways we have of accomplishing that God-given goal. Charles Swindoll, well-known pastor and author, composed an additional verse to the familiar old song, "Home on the Range," that captures this desire:

> "Oh give me a church
> Where the folks in the lurch
> Are encouraged and healed from above,
> Where seldom is heard
> A discouraging word,
> And the truth is modeled in love."

Wouldn't it be wonderful if church were a place where seldom was heard a discouraging word? I have actually had people say to me, "I go to church on Sunday, and it takes me all week to recover." I don't think that's the way God meant it to be. If the church of Jesus Christ is not a place where we can be who we are, and know that all throughout the process of our growth into maturity in the Lord we are going to be encouraged and motivated along the way by our fellow believers, then where would we go to find such a place? If not the church, where?

In this lesson, we're going to review a lot of Scripture that indicates just how much God intended for the church to be a center for mutual encouragement and edification. And especially how much encouragement was communicated by the apostles to the early church via the New Testament epistles. Their encouraging writings serve as a great model for learning to encourage people the "write way" today.

Recall for a moment some verses we have cited in previous lessons:

- Hebrews 10:24 "Let us consider and give attentive, continuous care to watching over one another, studying how we may stir up (stimulate and incite) to love and helpful deeds and noble activities." (The Amplified Bible)

- Hebrews 10:25 "Let us not neglect our church meetings as some people do, but encourage and warn each other, especially now that the day of His coming back again is drawing near." (The Living Bible)

- 1 Thessalonians 5:11, 14 "Therefore, comfort [encourage] each other and edify one another, just as you also are doing. Now we exhort you, brethren, warn those who are unruly, comfort [encourage] the fainthearted, uphold the weak, be patient with all."

That is the kind of place the church is to be—a place where sin is confronted, but people leave having been encouraged about the prospects of growing more mature in Christ. The challenges for living were serious in the New Testament day just as they are serious in our day.

I owe to Leland Barclay, a historian and authority on the use of words, a great insight concerning "encouragement." The Greek words for encouragement were used in nonbiblical writings of the day to describe the speeches military generals would give to their troops as they prepared to go into battle. They were encouraging and motivating their troops to give their all for the cause they were fighting for. And I thought to myself, "That's it!" That's what the church should be. We go into spiritual conflicts every day that manifest themselves in numbers of different ways in our lives. And we need to be encouraged. We need to have a transfusion of courage so that we can face the battles which are ours. Because we know that toward the end of history "perilous times will come" (2 Timothy 3:1), the need for encouragement grows greater day by day.

I believe one of the main reasons the New Testament epistles were written was to be a source of encouragement to the early church. When you think about what they were up against, you can easily imagine their need to be encouraged. Brand new churches were isolated geographically in distant parts of the Roman Empire at a time when the cruel emperor Nero was ruling. The only knowledge of Christianity they had was what they had been taught by the founding apostles—and perhaps through a scroll of the Old Testament if they happened to possess one. The first New Testament churches lived a delicate and tenuous existence, and Paul and the other apostles did everything they could in person and in writing to encourage them.

Let's look at a few examples of how Paul used encouraging words to build up the infant body of Christ (quoting from *The Living Bible*):

- Romans 1:8–9 "Let me say first of all that wherever I go I hear you being talked about! For your faith in God is becoming known around the world. How I thank God through Jesus Christ for this good report, and for each one of you. God knows how often I pray for you. Day and night I bring you and your needs in prayer to the One I serve with all of my might."

- 1 Corinthians 1:4–9 "I can never stop thanking God for all the wonderful gifts He has given you, now that you are Christ's: He has enriched your whole life. He has helped you to speak out for Him and has given you a full understanding of the truth; what I told you Christ could do for you has actually happened! Now you have every grace and blessing; every spiritual gift and power for doing His will . . . He guarantees right up to the end that you will be counted free from all sin and guilt on that day when He returns. God will surely do this for you, for He always does just what He says, and He is the One who invited you into this wonderful friendship with His Son, even Christ our Lord."

- 2 Corinthians 1:3–5 "What a wonderful God we have— He is the Father of our Lord Jesus Christ, the source of every mercy, and the One who so wonderfully comforts and strengthens us in our hardships and trials. And why does He do this? So that when others are troubled, needing our sympathy and encouragement, we can pass on to them this same help and comfort God has given to us. You can be sure that the more we undergo sufferings for Christ, the more He will shower us with His comfort and encouragement."

I can just imagine the early Christians receiving these letters from Paul and reading them over and over again just like we do when we receive an encouraging letter or note from someone. Most of the encouragement on which the church was built was in written form. We have good reason to believe that in many cases, Paul's letters would be copied by the receiving church and redistributed to others for their instruction and encouragement as well.

As I said in an earlier lesson, it is lamentable that we write as little as we do in this modern era; for I truly believe that written communication can be one of the most powerful forms of communication we have at our disposal. There are five reasons I believe written communication is far more valuable than spoken communication.

Written Encouragement Is Deliberate

Some people dispense a syrupy form of verbal "encouragement" non-stop when you are around them. It is often so profuse that it loses its meaning after a while. Like the old saying goes that can be applied to many things, "If everything is encouraging, then nothing is encouraging." Encouragement is far more meaningful when it is focused, specific, and deliberate. That's what makes written encouragement so meaningful.

Written encouragement demands a careful, prayerful, thoughtful investment of your time. You can walk around talking all day, but you can't walk around writing all day! Therefore, when you receive a written note or letter from someone, you know they took the time to sit down and write to you on purpose. The phrase, "It's not the gift, it's the journey," applies to written communication. While you may deeply appreciate what the person had to say in their note to you, the fact that they took the time to write is just as meaningful.

In the mountains above where I live in California is a small town called Julian. The Julian Pie Factory turns out pies that are famous all around our area. One day I drove to Julian, bought twenty of those beautiful pies and brought them home and gave them away to friends. That's a good example of "It's not the gift, it's the journey." While the pies are delicious, the better part of the gift is the fact that the pie came from Julian, high up in the California mountains. To receive a Julian Pie Factory pie is to receive all the romanticism and fun of knowing where it came from.

The same is true when you receive a written word of encouragement from someone. The journey they took to get their word to you means as much as the word itself.

Written Encouragement Is Definite

Every one of us has meant to write a note or speak a word of encouragement that we just never quite got around to taking care of. We couldn't find a pen, we didn't have a stamp, we lost their address, we had all their address except the zip code, and our computer crashed when we tried to go to the Postal Service web site to get the zip code. I know how it goes. There are all kinds of reasons that our words of encouragement remain at the level of good intentions.

We are so free with our words—"Let's get together some time!" "Let's have lunch!" "We need to have you all over for supper!" "Let's get our families together at the lake!"—that we say far more than we actually mean. But a written letter or note of encouragement is undeniable. It is living proof, held in your hands, that you definitely are sending a word of encouragement to a friend. And if you receive something written, it definitely means that another person cared enough about you not just to intend to encourage you but to actually do it.

Another great aspect of written communication is that you can do it any time. You don't have to wait to run into the person or hope you can reach them by phone. Nothing can stop you from encouraging a person by writing—when you drop it in the mailbox, it's done!

WRITTEN ENCOURAGEMENT IS DIRECT

Why, you may ask, is written encouragement more direct than spoken encouragement? In my experience, it is more direct because you are free from the face-to-face intimidation and inhibition factors that plague the human race. It's unfortunate but true. We often have a difficult time even looking one another in the eye, much less saying what is really on our heart. That's not always the case, but it certainly occurs at times. In person, we are often afraid to say to people what we would really like for them to know—how much we appreciate them, how much we admire what they did, how sorry we are for the suffering they have experienced. Sometimes we hold back because we don't want to make them feel uncomfortable in our presence.

Even the great apostle Paul said that he could be more bold when he wasn't with the Corinthians in person: "I, Paul . . . am lowly among you, but being absent am bold toward you" (2 Corinthians 10:1). Paul was weak and lowly in many ways, though he could be bold when the situation called for it. When it came to calling the Corinthians on the carpet, he preferred to do that in written form rather than to confront them face-to-face. He wanted to spare their humiliation.

Written communication gives us the opportunity to exhort (remember: exhortation can be a form of encouragement) or praise or build up without reservation. There are no insecurities or barriers keeping us from being as direct as we want or need to be.

Written Encouragement Is Durable

Let's face it—paper is more durable than our fading memories. When someone speaks a word of encouragement to you, especially if it makes an emotional impact, you'll remember it for a long time—perhaps most of your adult life. But if there's something you want to be preserved for a lifetime, write it down. As someone has said, "If it's not in writing, it doesn't exist."

I still have the very first note of encouragement I ever received. The paper is yellowed and getting brittle, but I can still read it. It is dated February 26, 1941, just 13 days after I was born. It was written to me by a man who was a spiritual mentor to my father. He pastored the church my father ultimately pastored, was president of a Bible college, and a godly saint of a man. Here is part of the note he wrote to me when I was just 13 days old:

"Master David Paul Jeremiah: My Dear David, It is quite beyond me to tell you how glad I am to welcome you to our country, to my native state, to dear old Toledo, Ohio, and to the Emmanuel Baptist Church, to the parsonage where we spent so many delightful years, and to the alumni of the Bible Baptist Seminary . . . Here is hoping that you will live up to your name, as I am confident you will. You certainly made the best possible choice as to parentage. And you can well follow in the footsteps of your mother on everything, even as to appearance, and of your father on everything, except the matter of attention given to your hair. It is better to comb it occasionally.

"Here's hoping that your dad is as well as can be expected. My best to your lassie sister, to your neighbors, to all our good friends at Emmanuel . . . Happy days and many of them. The Lord bless you."

I share part of that little personal note just to prove how durable words of encouragement are. I'm sure you have similar examples in your own files or scrapbooks. But rather than marvel at the "good old days" when all people had was the U.S. mail, we should realize just how valuable and durable written words are and imitate those earlier generations of writers.

WRITTEN ENCOURAGEMENT IS DISTANCE-PROOF

A final point—written communication knows no boundaries of time or geography. Veteran missionaries in remote corners of the world tell us that the most important day is when an airplane or helicopter brings supplies—and most importantly, the mail from home. People who are separated from loved ones either by time or distance can rely on written communication to keep them linked to their most important sources of encouragement—those who love and care for them.

If you are not a writer of notes of encouragement, may I encourage you to begin? Your deliberate, definite, direct, durable, and distance-proof words may supply the transfusion of courage that a weary heart needs today—and into the future.

1. Read Titus 1:1–9.

   a. What are the two descriptive terms Paul gives himself in verse 1?

   b. What is Paul's hope? When was it established? (verse 2)

   c. Explain why verse 3 elevates preaching to such a high and critical role in our faith.

   d. Who is this letter written to? How does Paul describe him? (verse 4)

   e. What three things does Paul pray upon his friend? From what source? (verse 4)

   f. Why do you think Paul gave such a long introduction to this letter? Do you think it left Titus encouraged? Why or why not?

2. Read James 1:1–20.

   a. To whom is this letter addressed?

   b. James encourages Christians to rejoice at what? (verse 2) Why? (verse 3)

   c. What is your initial reaction to verses 2–3 being the first sentence in this letter?

   d. Explain why the early church's response to this opening was probably different than yours.

   e. What are the fruits of patience in the life of a believer? (verse 4)

   f. What should we do when we need wisdom? (verse 5) Why is that seldom our first reaction?

   g. In what two ways will God give to us? (verse 5)

h. In what way do we need to ask? Why? (verse 6)

i. Why won't God give to a doubting believer? (verse 8)

j. Based on this opening paragraph, hypothesize and list some of the issues that were facing believers at this time.

k. Are these issues relevant to us today? Why or why not?

3. Read Jude 1:1–4.
   a. Who is the letter written for? (verse 1)

   b. What is Jude's prayer for this group of people? (verse 2)

   c. What are two reasons why Jude wrote this letter? (verse 3)

d. What is the serious problem facing the church? (verse 4) Is this still relevant today? Explain.

4. Look back and review to whom Titus, James, and Jude were written. What is striking about this? What does this tell you about God's Word? About God?

DID YOU KNOW?

When people talk about the Epistles in the Bible, many actually don't understand what that term really means. The word *epistle* is the Greek word for "letter." The Epistles were literally letters written to the various churches, mainly by Paul. So it is good to remember that when we refer to the sixty-six books of the Bible that we don't overlook the diversity of styles and structures in those books. Some are songs and poems (like the Psalms), some are narratives (like Genesis) and some are letters (like Ephesians). They may be different in size, scope, and structure, but they are all the inspired Word of God.

WITH FRIENDS LIKE THESE

Job 2:11

In this lesson we learn how not *to be an encourager.*

OUTLINE

You're feeling down and discouraged and a "friend" comes along who proceeds to outline the cause and cure of your troubles. If you just follow his advice, you'll be fine. By the time he leaves, you're not only still discouraged, but wrestling with anger as well.

  I.   **They Responded to Job's Words, but Failed to Feel His Pain**

 II.   **They Refused to Recognize Suffering as Part of God's Plan**

III.   **They Related All of Job's Suffering to Sin in His Life**

IV.   **They Reacted by Failing to See the Uniqueness of Job's Suffering**

I n our study, we have said in a number of ways that one of the greatest needs we have in our culture today is the need for encouragement—the transfusion of courage from one person to another—especially in the lives of our young people. It only stands to reason that if we have a great need for encouragement that there must be a lot of discouragement going on to create that situation. And that is true.

In the Bible, we have a three-fold example of discouragement—the art of bleeding the courage right out of a person weakened by circumstances or suffering. And that example is found in the book of Job in the Old Testament. Everyone is familiar with the story of Job, but one aspect of it we are less familiar with is the role played by Job's three friends who came (supposedly) to help him in his hour of need.

The first chapter of the book tells us how Satan came into God's presence and said he had been walking upon the earth. God asked him if he had considered (noticed, observed) Job, what a righteous man he was. Satan said it was not surprising that Job feared God because God protected Job from all harm. So God told Satan he could remove all Job's possessions to prove that Job's fear of the Lord was not based on his blessings. God was not tempting or testing Job, but rather creating an opportunity for Job to demonstrate his integrity to Satan and his hosts.

So God removed the hedge from around Job, and Satan removed all of Job's possessions. Thousands of head of livestock were killed or stolen, and all ten of his children were killed. Most of his servants were also destroyed. In fact, everything Job had was taken from him except his wife (Job 1:13–19). And how did Job respond? Perfectly, as God predicted:

"Naked I came from my mother's womb, and naked shall I return there. The Lord gave, and the Lord has taken away; blessed be the name of the Lord. In all this Job did not sin nor charge God with wrong" (Job 1:21–22).

Satan returned to God and said, "If You will give me access to Job's physical health, I can make him deny You." God granted Satan permission, with the caveat that he must not take Job's life. Here are all the afflictions the Bible says Job was struck with at the hand of Satan: Terrible itching, insomnia, running sores and scabs, nightmares, weight loss, chills and fever, diarrhea, and blackened skin that literally fell off of his body. His physical condition was so drastic that when his friends came to visit him, they didn't even recognize him (Job 2:12). Even his wife appears to have turned on him, encouraging him to curse God and die—to just get it over with (Job 2:9).

But in spite of his suffering, Job rejected his wife's counsel and remained true to God:

"You speak as one of the foolish women speaks. Shall we indeed accept good from God, and shall we not accept adversity? In all this Job did not sin with his lips" (Job 2:10).

When three of Job's friends hear of his affliction, they start off on the right foot by coming to console him. In spite of the discouragement they ultimately offer, we have to give them credit for at least coming to their friend when they heard he was in trouble. They came to mourn with Job and to comfort him, and they sat with him for seven days and nights without speaking a word. They tore their robes and mourned and wept for their friend Job at the great misfortune that had befallen him (Job 2:11–13). They did a number of encouraging things: They came to where their friend was, they wept for him, they identified with him by sitting in the ash heap alongside him. And the wisest thing they did was not to say a word for a week. Actually, they would have been wiser had they not spoken at all; for when they spoke, they caused more harm than good.

We get a picture of the kind of encouragement they gave Job by turning to Job 16:1–5. In short, Job says, "You guys are a miserable bunch of encouragers! If you were in my place, at least I would try to comfort you with words that would relieve your grief." Perhaps you have encountered a modern day Eliphaz, Bildad, or Zophar—people who take it upon themselves to straighten you out in your hour of misery. If so, then you know how Job felt. Let's meet these three pseudo-encouragers up close and personal.

Eliphaz was the first to speak, and appropriately so since he was the oldest. His favorite phrase is, "I have seen." He loves to explain Job's misery in terms of what he has observed in his long life. In addition to his observations from life, he puts great stock in a dream he had one night, the main message of which was that no man is more righteous than God (Job 4:12–21). The upshot of that in Job's case must be that Job is unrighteous; he has done something bad to deserve the misfortune he is experiencing. He summarizes his point of view for Job by asking him,

"Remember now, who ever perished being innocent? Or where were the upright ever cut off? (Job 4:7).

Wouldn't that have been an encouragement to Job? To have a "friend" come and say, "Look, Job, no one who is upright ever goes through this kind of trouble. God doesn't punish the righteous. If you're reaping suffering, you must have sown sin—so let's get to the bottom line: What have you done that has caused God to punish you like this?" Far too often, well-meaning Christian friends have a way of creating false guilt among those who are suffering. We have a biblical theology that says God is going to one day punish the sins of the wicked—and He is. But then we take that theology and apply it across the board and assume that every time someone suffers, it is because God is punishing them.

In Job's case, we know that he wasn't suffering because he was bad. To the contrary, we are told by God himself that Job was suffering because he was good. His experience has been orchestrated and allowed by God in order to demonstrate his integrity and uprightness. So immediately we know that Eliphaz is wrong in his judgment of Job.

Next comes Bildad. If I had to use an analogy to illustrate Bildad's approach to Job, I would compare him to a Pharisee in Jesus' day. That is, Bildad was a legalist. Job 8:20 has a summary statement of Bildad's point of view: "Behold, God will not cast away the blameless, nor will He uphold the evildoers." Again, the implication to Job is, "You're in this mess because of your sin." In fact, after Bildad has inserted the proverbial knife, he gives it a twist: "If your sons have sinned against [God], He has cast them away for their transgression" (Job 8:4). Not only have you sinned, Bildad suggests, but your ten children are dead because they sinned, too. What an encourager Bildad is!

The youngest of the three takes his turn next. Zophar is like the young preacher or counselor fresh out of school who thinks he knows all the answers. He begins his words by saying, "Know this." Here's a young buck talking to one of his elders saying, "Know this, Job." It makes you not even want to hear what he has to say, doesn't it? And his arrogance extends beyond his introduction. His perspective can be summed up by the words in Job 11:6b: "Know therefore that God exacts from you less than your iniquity deserves." Ouch! Not only do you deserve this, Job, but much more. Remember, Job has lost everything but his pulse and his foul-smelling breath (Job 19:17), yet Zophar says he deserves to lose much more. Isn't Zophar a blessing?

Job was accosted by three men who should have known that he wasn't in misery because of his sin—yet he had to sit on the ash heap and receive their discouraging words. We ought to pray that God would keep such discouragers away from us should He ever orchestrate a Job-like day for us. Let's look at four principles we can extract from the erroneous efforts of these three friends of Job.

THEY RESPONDED TO JOB'S WORDS, BUT FAILED TO FEEL HIS PAIN

Job is a long and involved book to read, but if you work your way through all the exchanges between Job and his three friends, you discover this: They really weren't hearing what Job was saying. They responded to his words, not to him. Sometimes you can be in a conversation with someone and you realize that the whole time you are talking, they are not listening to you. Instead, they are preparing what they are planning to say next. Their goal is not to hear you, but to make sure you hear them.

When we approach someone who is suffering, it is so easy to go with preconceived ideas about their situation. They usually need for us to do what Job's friends did before they started talking—just be there to comfort them.

In an earlier lesson, I mentioned Joseph Bayly who buried three of his sons. Here is what he said about two different people who came to see him when one of his sons died:

"I was sitting, torn by grief. Someone came and talked to me of God's dealings and why it happened, of hope beyond the grave. He talked constantly. He said things I knew were true. I was unmoved except to wish he'd go away. He finally did. Another came and sat beside me. He just sat beside me for an hour and more. Listened when I said something, answered briefly, prayed simply, and left. I was moved. I was encouraged. I hated to see him go."

THEY REFUSED TO RECOGNIZE SUFFERING AS PART OF GOD'S PLAN

I could not find one piece of evidence that Job's three friends thought God's plan could ever include suffering for the righteous. Yet, as we study Job's experience, we have to conclude that God was at work for good purposes in his life. Not only was the current state of Job's integrity being demonstrated, but God was at work perfecting him, taking him to a higher (deeper) level of spiritual maturity. To fail to recognize this in the life of someone who is suffering is to be guilty of the same immaturity as were Job's friends.

Many of the Psalms, and much of the rest of Scripture, are devoted to describing the experiences of believers whose backs are against the wall, who are in some kind of pain. Unlike Job, who maintained his innocence, the person in that situation is often the first to think he has done something to offend God. Often it takes a friend to provide an objective viewpoint—to remind the sufferer that God may be at work for a different and deeper reason. It has struck me in doing this study that too often we pray for God to release the sufferer from his pain instead of praying, "God, show us what you are doing in this person's life. Help me be an encouragement to him while Your purposes are accomplished, whatever they are, in this person's life."

Living in the "health and wealth" culture of twenty-first century America, we need especially to guard against the nonbiblical mentality that suffering can never be part of God's plan. There have been too many martyrs—and there are an increasing number of modern martyrs—in the history of the church for such a concept possibly to be true. As encouragers, we need to ask God for wisdom and insight before we make judgments.

THEY RELATED ALL OF JOB'S SUFFERING TO SIN IN HIS LIFE

As encouragers, we need to be careful about making a distinction about sin and suffering that is clearly biblical: All suffering is due to sin, but not all individual experiences of suffering are due to individual guilt of sin. True, if Adam and Eve had never sinned in the Garden of Eden, then we would know no suffering in this life. Indeed, there will be no suffering in heaven where God restores creation to its order of glory and perfection in the new heaven and new earth (Revelation 21:4).

Job's friends crossed the theological line when they assumed that Job's individual experience of suffering was due to his individual sin. Can you imagine the grief that is caused a person who is already hurting when he hears that? A young woman in our church told me that when her mother died of cancer twenty years ago, a pastor told her that her mother had not had enough faith to be healed and that there had been sin in her life. Thankfully, I was able to show her from the Scriptures why that was not true. But she had lived with that grief for twenty years, wondering what her mother had done that had caused her not to be healed. If that is the only word of encouragement you have to offer someone, it would be better not to speak at all.

THEY REACTED BY FAILING TO SEE THE UNIQUENESS OF JOB'S SUFFERING

The last thing we need to note about Job's three friends is how they failed to treat Job as a unique individual, as a person. They came with their prepackaged theological perspectives which lump all people into the sin-and-suffer camp. There was no room in their theory for Job or anyone else to be going through a situation in which God was doing a unique thing.

I have come to understand that every experience of suffering is totally unique to the person who is experiencing it. It is unique in the sense that it is this suffering for this person at this particular time in this particular context—and there is no way you or I could know how they feel. We can tell them we care for them and that we want to know how they are feeling if they want to tell us. But we cannot walk in and tell the answer to their situation (which presumes we know the cause and how they are feeling about it). It's perfectly acceptable simply to say, "I don't know," and reveal our own vulnerability by declaring ourselves, along with the sufferer, one who simply must wait upon God.

Christian encouragement is more an art than a science. There is not a formula to follow. Rather, we must be sensitive to the leading of the Spirit and to the needs of our hurting friend. If the most we can do is simply be there, it will be enough if we do it in the power of the Spirit.

APPLICATION

1. Read Proverbs 14:6–7.

   a. Why do you think it is hard for a scoffer to find wisdom?

   b. What are we to do when we encounter a foolish person? (verse 7)

   c. How will we be able to spot a foolish person? (verse 7)

2. Read Romans 16:17–18.

   a. Paul bids us to note people who cause what two things? (verse 17)

b. What are we to do with them? (verse 17)

c. Whom do such people serve? (verse 18)

d. What are their methods of deception? (verse 18)

e. Why do you think Paul advises us to avoid them rather than confront them?

3. Read 1 Corinthians 15:33–34.

a. Paraphrase verse 33 into your own words. How does this apply to your life?

b. What two commandments are we given? (verse 34)

c. What do those two commandments in verse 34 have to do with the evil company mentioned in verse 33?

d. What do some people lack altogether? (verse 34)

e. List some ways that Christians can be witnesses to the godless without compromise or corruption.

4. Read Philippians 1:12–18.

a. What is Paul's conclusion to the trials that have beset him? (verse 12)

b. How does he interpret his prison experience? (verse 13)

c. What has been the blessed result of Paul bearing chains? (verse 14)

d. What are the two ways in which some preach Christ? (verse 15)

e. What is the perspective on Paul by those who preach out of selfish ambition? (verse 16)

f. Those who preach out of love understand what about Paul? (verse 17)

g. No matter the method, what is Paul's greatest passion? (verse 18)

h. If Christ is preached, what can Paul truly say even from a prison cell? (verse 18)

DID YOU KNOW?

Jesus did not send His disciples and followers to do His work alone. Mark 6:7 tells us that Jesus sent His disciples "out two by two." And in Luke 10:1, "the Lord appointed seventy others also, and sent them two by two before His face into every city and place where He Himself was about to go." This shows the importance of having companions and friends to share life with—especially in ministry. And it only underscores how crucial and critical it is that we are careful in our choice of friends, lest we compromise and lose our testimony.

It's Up to You and Me, Friend

Romans 12:3–21

*In this lesson we learn how the church works
to encourage itself and the world.*

OUTLINE

In the human body, every limb, organ, and cell works to contribute
what it can to the overall health of the whole. Paul likens the church
to a body with individual Christians being responsible to do their
part to encourage (strengthen) the whole.

I. **The Immensity of the Church**

II. **The Unity of the Church**

III. **The Diversity of the Church**

IV. **The Interdependency of the Church**

V. **The Responsibility of the Church**

VI. **The Characteristics of the Church**
    A. Encouragers Will Be Genuine
    B. Encouragers Will Be Assertive
    C. Encouragers Will Be Selfless
    D. Encouragers Will Be Humble

A strange set of statistics has surfaced in America in the last decade. More people than ever are claiming to be religious, but church attendance and interest overall has declined. What does that say? It means that a lot of people don't think they need to be part of the local church in order to have a healthy relationship with God. The idea has gained strength that it's okay to be a floating Christian, a Christian-at-large, taking advantage of the benefits the church brings to communities and the culture without wanting to be part of it.

A number of reasons might be cited for why people are staying away from church. But I believe one of the most important is that people just don't see it as a place that is going to add a dimension of health and encouragement to their lives. We know people in society need encouraging today. Just look around and you'll see lots of reasons why peoples' hearts are "failing them from fear" (Luke 21:26). If they need strength and courage, why don't they see the church as a place where they can find it?

The apostle Paul gives a blueprint for the kind of church where every person is an encourager—and that's the kind of church to which those who need encouraging will come. His blueprint is found where he discusses spiritual gifts, the two most extensive passages being Romans 12 and 1 Corinthians 12. I mentioned in a previous lesson that of the fifteen or so "one another" passages in the New Testament, five of them specifically have to do with encouragement. And when we look at Paul's instructions to the body of Christ in Romans 12 concerning spiritual gifts and their ministry in the body, we will see how important it is for every person to be an encourager.

In Romans 12:3–8, Paul says in no uncertain terms that every member of the body has been given "a measure of faith" by God. And that measure of faith is a spiritual gift, given to be used by the recipient for the strengthening (the building up and encouraging, the edifying) of the rest of the church. This doctrine comes as a surprise to many Christians when they hear it for the first time. They believe there is a line of demarcation in the church that runs between the pulpit and the first pew. They think that everything important and of a service nature that happens takes place on the pulpit side of the line, and everything of a spectator or observational sort takes place on the pew side of the line.

Nothing could be further from the truth of God's Word. First, there is no line of demarcation between the clergy and the laity. Instead of a line separating the two, there is a large circle which encompasses all true believers, pastors and members alike. The only difference between pastors and nonpastors is in gifts and roles. But each member of the body has gifts and roles that are as important as every other member's. Only when every member of the body of Christ becomes an active participant in the ministry of the church will it become the living, organic source of encouragement God intends it to be.

There are six aspects of the body of Christ which call for every member to be an active employer of the spiritual gifts he has been given.

THE IMMENSITY OF THE CHURCH

The first thing to note about the church is its sheer size: "We have many members in one body." He is speaking, of course, about the entire body of Christ worldwide, not any one local congregation. There are many, many Christians in the church of Jesus Christ, "but all the members do not have the same function" (Romans 12:4).

Because God has given every single believer a measure of faith that is manifested in spiritual gifts, He intends for every single believer to be involved in building up and strengthening the body of Christ around the world. God never intended for there to be someone at the top of the church structure worldwide who takes care of all the ministry. Nor does He intend for that to be the case at the local church level. Local churches are not usually "immense," but the same principle still applies. There are far too many people in the average local church for any pastor or staff to be able to care for by themselves. And in the age of mega-churches that we live in, it is all the more true. Unless each believer is involved in using his gift to build up the body of Christ, church will be a discouraging, rather than encouraging, place to be.

Every time a person in the body of Christ says, "It's not my responsibility to encourage that person," that means somebody in that church isn't getting the ministry God intended them to receive. So unique is God's idea of spiritual gifts that it doesn't matter how big the church gets—there will always be enough "ministers" to take care of it. The members are the ministers.

The Unity of the Church

Next, Paul says that the many members of the church are united "in one body." Just as the human body has individual limbs and organs that perform certain functions yet are attached and unified, so does the body of Christ. Diversity yet unity is the way to describe the church.

To use an athletic metaphor, believers are on the same team, striving for the same goal. Spiritual gifts are given by God to strengthen individuals, but with the team in mind. As individual members are encouraged and built up, the church at large is made stronger and healthier. And as that happens, those in society who are less healthy will be drawn to the church as a source of strength. Think of it— why would any person be drawn to an organism that seems less healthy than the person is? Wasn't Jesus Christ's emotional, spiritual, and physical health part of His uniqueness? Surely people recognized in Him a human being unlike others in society. He spoke with authority, He was wise, He was healthy, He was unruffled by the social and political turmoil of His day.

Granted, each individual in the body of Christ is important in God's sight. But as each individual member is made healthy, the body is made healthy. Every member ought to see it as his goal to encourage the part of the body of Christ he belongs to.

The Diversity of the Church

The body of Christ is large, yet it is one. That brings into focus the diversity of the body of Christ. Not only are we diverse in the spiritual gifts God has given to each one, but we are diverse in many other ways as well. It is plainly obvious that no one can minister to everyone! Even if I had the time or strength to minister to everyone in our large church, it would not be wise for me to do so. I simply will not "connect" with every other individual in a meaningful way. Number one, I don't have all the spiritual gifts needed; and number two, I don't have the personality, gender, ethnic background, or education to relate ideally with every other person. That is why every person in the body of Christ needs to be an encourager. There is somebody in the body who can connect with another person in terms of giftedness and personality until everyone is connected to someone.

There are divorced people in the church. There are families with children who have physical or mental challenges. There are people with extreme financial needs. There are people struggling in their marriages. There are people discouraged about their vocations. There are people facing life-threatening illnesses. There are people trapped in moral sins and addictions. The church is like a kaleidoscope in two ways: It's incredibly varied when you look at it in a moment in time; but it never looks the same way twice. Your church today is not the church you attended yesterday, nor is it the church you will attend tomorrow. Things are happening to people every minute of every day that radically impact their lives and make their needs different. And because their needs and experiences change, their ability to minister on the basis of what they've learned changes as well (2 Corinthians 1:3–4). Someone who experiences a crisis in January and comes out the other side of it in March becomes qualified to be an encourager to someone who enters a similar crisis in April. The body of Christ is so diverse and changes so rapidly that it is imperative that every member be active in building it up.

THE INTERDEPENDENCY OF THE CHURCH

When Paul says we are "individually members of one another" (Romans 12:5), he is saying that, in spite of our uniqueness, we are connected. In fact, not only are we connected, we are dependent on one another. Just as the human body grows weak as individual organs begin to malfunction or shut down, so does the body of Christ. We simply cannot afford not to have every member doing that which God has called him to do.

My friend, Pastor Kent Hughes, talks about the plague of ecclesiastical hitchhikers in today's church. Hitchhikers want you to buy the car, pay for the gas and insurance, and keep it well maintained—but let them ride in it. It's the same way with some Christians. They're happy to let someone else keep the church well-oiled and running smoothly so they can drop in and drop out as their schedule allows or their needs dictate. George Barna, the Christian pollster, agrees with that assessment. He has said, "The average adult thinks that belonging to a church is good for other people, but represents unnecessary bondage and baggage for himself."[1]

Someone has said the church has two kinds of people in it: The pillars and the caterpillars. The pillars hold the church up so the caterpillars can crawl in and out every Sunday. And in some ways, that's as it should be. Not everyone at every time is strong enough to hold the church up; some are barely strong enough to get themselves to church at all. But overall, we have far too many people who are healthy but just don't see the need or relevance for being involved. If you're not involved, you're not connected.

THE RESPONSIBILITY OF THE CHURCH

Finally, Paul says, "Having then gifts differing according to the grace that is given to us, let us use them" (Romans 12:6). This is the bottom line, isn't it? If we are to encourage those in the body of Christ who need encouraging—not to mention those in our culture who are weak and searching for the relief for their souls only Jesus can give—somebody is going to have to become an encourager! This will not happen because we talk about it or plan for it; it will only happen when we begin to use the gifts God has given for that very purpose.

When I preached on this subject in our church, people came up to me during the series and said, "You've been spending a lot of time on application in this series of sermons." My reply? "You'd better believe it!" If we don't start getting past the sanctified veneers that we wear to church each Sunday and begin to reveal who we are and what our needs are—and then use the gifts God has given to encourage the discouraged—we are just playing church instead of being the church. We are responsible, before God first and before one another second, to use that with which we have been entrusted.

THE CHARACTERISTICS OF THE CHURCH

What will characterize a church that has decided to use its gifts to encourage and build up the body of Christ? Four things:

Encouragers Will Be Genuine

First of all, good encouragers have to be genuine people. You can't be phony and expect anyone to be encouraged by you. Paul says in verse 9, "Let love be without hypocrisy." Encouragers won't fake it; they'll be real—and people will be attracted to their genuineness.

Encouragers Will Be Assertive

Lest you think I am adopting a characteristic of the world system, look at some of the words Paul uses in this section of verses: "Not lagging," "fervent," "cling to," "given to." In verse 13, the phrase "given to hospitality" literally means "pursuing hospitality." Believers who are encouragers will be assertive, especially in pursuing hospitality. One of the problems in our churches is that everyone thinks that someone else is taking care of the people who have needs. If everyone thinks that, it means no one is taking care of anyone. Instead of everyone thinking that someone else is doing the encouraging, here is what every believer should think: No one is taking care of anyone, therefore I have to take care of everyone I can. It's not true that no one is caring for people, but I use that extreme statement to illustrate the fact that we can't sit back. We have to step up and assume that if I don't do it, it won't get done.

If you're going to err, err on the side of being a little too aggressive. If one person is invited to lunch after church by three separate people, that's a whole lot better than not being invited by anyone.

Encouragers Will Be Selfless

Paul's words in verses 14 and 15 are meant to get us out of who we are and into who someone else is. We are far too absorbed in our world—our needs, our schedule, our failures, our weaknesses. Encouraging people and getting involved in their lives is a lot like having children. If you wait until you can afford it, are wise enough to be a parent, and have time to raise kids, you'll never have children. You just have to get out of yourself and into another person's life whether you feel ready, able, equipped, or not. And usually you feel "not."

Encouragers Will Be Humble

Finally, verse 16, encouragers will be humble. If you're the kind of person who only wants to reach out to people like yourself (people who "have it together"), then we have a way to go. We need to reach out to every person who has a need—lovely or unlovely (just as we are often unlovely in our lives, and God reaches out to us).

The church of Jesus Christ is where God wants the world to come to be built up from the ravages of sin and darkness. The best way for us to shine a light on the threshold of the kingdom is for us to welcome them and one another with open arms that say, "Come in. Let me give you a little bit of the courage God has given me." That's what it means to be an encourager in the body of Christ today.

Note:

1. George Barna, *Baby Busters, The Disillusioned Generation* (Chicago: Northfield Publishing, 1992).

1. Read Psalm 89:5–7.

   a. In what two places is God's faithfulness proclaimed? (verse 5)

   b. Why is God worthy of our praise? (verse 6)

   c. The church is not only to praise God, but also to hold what two attitudes before Him? (verse 7)

   d. Out of the commands to praise, fear, and revere God, which one does the modern church do the best job of following? The worst? Explain why for both answers.

2. Read Psalm 111:1.

   a. How are we to praise God?

   b. In what two places are we to praise God?

   c. Explain the subtle difference between those two places and why the psalmist designated them both.

3. Read Acts 20:28–32.

   a. Who are we to oversee? (verse 28)

   b. Who made us overseers? (verse 28)

c. What was the church built upon? (verse 28)

d. What are we to watch for in the church? (verse 29)

e. What is the purpose of these wolves in the church? (verse 30)

f. How long did Luke warn about this coming attack? (verse 31)

g. What alone is able to build up the church in this fight? (verse 32)

4. Read 1 Corinthians 3:9 –11.

   a. The workers of God are given two names. Name them. (verse 9)

   b. What do you think it means to be God's building? God's field?

   c. Why was Paul able to build the church's foundation? (verse 10)

   d. What does Paul then warn us about? (verse 10)

e. What is the only foundation of the church? (verse 11)

f. Describe some foundations that modern churches try to apply other than Christ.

4. Read James 2: 1–4.

   a. Why is partiality and favoritism in the church such an offense to God?

   b. How can you help combat this problem in your church this coming Sunday?

DID YOU KNOW?

God's marvelous power has rarely been in greater display than in His creation and formation of the church. Recall that before the Lord appeared to Paul, he was Saul, a devout Jew who "persecuted the church of God beyond measure and tried to destroy it" (Galatians 1:13). But God not only thwarted Saul's plans to destroy His church, He converted him and made him an instrument to build, lead, and guide the church. The apostle Paul's epistles did nothing less than lay the framework for the faith that we share today. Only God could orchestrate a miracle like that!

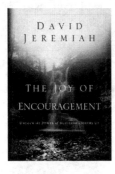

The Joy of Encouragement
Unlock the Power of Building Others Up

Dr. Jeremiah examines the heart of self-giving, genuine love—and suggests helpful ways to learn to express the kind of encouragement that heals, unites, and renews peoples' zest for life. Scriptural and uplifting, *The Joy of Encouragement* has the potential to radically reshape the world and to equip people as ambassadors of the God of love.

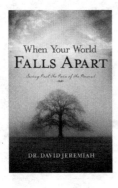

When Your World Falls Apart
Seeing Past the Pain of the Present

When life suddenly turns upside down, there, in the midst of your trials and in the center of your pain is God—comforting, guiding, encouraging, teaching, sustaining. In this perceptive and deeply personal book, David Jeremiah draws from the beautiful poetry and deep truths of the Psalms—passages that gave him comfort and strength on his journey into the unknown. Interwoven with his own reflections and insights are the inspiring real-life stories of other men and women who have faced unexpected adversity—and found God's grace sufficient for every need.

God in You
Releasing the Power of the Holy Spirit in Your Life

If you belong to Jesus Christ, He—God's Spirit—is in you. This mighty Resident within will change your life beyond anything you might dream. In this book, Dr. Jeremiah not only lays the biblical foundation for understanding the Spirit's multiple ministries, he also shows how this "forgotten Member of the Trinity" can transform a marriage, a parent, a church, a relationship at work, and attitudes toward life itself.

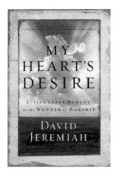

My Heart's Desire
Living Every Moment in the Wonder of Worship

In *My Heart's Desire*, Dr. David Jeremiah shares how you can experience an exuberant passion for God every moment of your life. Dr. Jeremiah invites you to discover a fresh understanding worship, exploring what it means to encounter God every day with a heart filled with marvel and praise.

For pricing information and ordering, contact us at

P.O. Box 3838
San Diego, CA 92163
(800) 947-1993
WWW.DAVIDJEREMIAH.ORG

STAY CONNECTED
TO DR. DAVID JEREMIAH

Take advantage of two great ways to let Dr. David Jeremiah give you spiritual direction every day! Both are absolutely FREE.

Turning Points Magazine and Devotional

Receive Dr. David Jeremiah's monthly magazine, *Turning Points* each month:

- Monthly study focus
- 48 pages of life-changing reading
- Relevant articles
- Special features
- Humor section
- Family section
- Daily devotional readings for each day of the month
- Bible study resource offers
- Live event schedule
- Radio & television information

Your Daily Turning Point E-Devotional

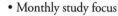

Start your day off right! Find words of inspiration and spiritual motivation waiting for you on your computer every morning! You can receive a daily e-devotion communication from David Jeremiah that will strengthen your walk with God and encourage you to live the authentic Christian life.

There are two easy ways to sign up for these free resources from Turning Point. Visit us online at www.DavidJeremiah.org and select "Subscribe to Daily Devotional by Email" or visit the home page and find Daily Devotional to subscribe to your monthly copy of *Turning Points*.